GOD
CALLED ME...

I'll Be Damned If I Don't Preach!

Dr. Willie D. McClung

Columbus, GA

Copyright © 2022 by Willie D. McClung

All rights reserved. No part of this publication may be reproduced, distributed, or transmitted in any form or by any means, including photocopying, recording, digital scanning, or other electronic or mechanical methods, without the prior written permission of the publisher, and author, except in the case of brief quotations embodied in critical reviews and certain other noncommercial uses permitted by copyright law. Unlawful use without permission is prohibited by copyright law. For permission requests, please address:

Tidan Publishing LLC
P.O. Box 9482
Columbus, Georgia 31907
Tidanpublishingllc@gmail.com

Distributed by Tidan Publishing LLC
Cover Design & Illustrations by Dr. Willie McClung and Tidan Publishing

Illustrations in book contents are copyrighted and used by permission and purchased licensing from Shutterstock.

Scriptures marked as King James Version are taken from the King James Bible, public domain.

Published 2022
Columbus, Georgia
Printed in the United States of America
ISBN 978-1-7368173-2-2

Library of Congress Control Number: Pending

Dedication

Thanks to my mother, the cause of it all, and the memory of my father, whose life is so deeply embedded in my heart.

Thanks to my wife Mary Jean, who encouraged me to put my thoughts in writing.

Thanks to my five children: David, Rosemary, Bonita, RaShon and LaDawn, who serve as a back-up to undiscovered knowledge.

Table of Contents

Introduction 1
Words in Season 3
God Has Made of One Blood, All Nations 11
When God Seems Distant 21
The Anchor of the Soul 27
Life's Eraser 35
The Benefits of Being in God's Family 45
Fainting In The Day of Adversity 55
Small Things 63
Holding On and Growing Stronger 73
The Harvest is Ripe 83
The Anakims 93
Our Everlasting Father 103
A Man of Sorrow, Acquainted With Grief 111
God's Design of Men 119
The Marks of Jesus 127
Toiling All Night and Taking Nothing 137
Human Wreckage 147
Ask What I Shall Give Thee 157
Judging Prematurely 165
Life's Blessings 177
Conquerors Through Christ 185
Man's Lack of Knowledge of Himself 195
The Obligation to Persevere 205
Equal Sacrifices 215
A Good Mother 225
Acknowledgements 233
About The Author 235

✝ Introduction

In March of 2020, the Governor of the State of Alabama went on television to announce the closure of all state and city operations. Schools, businesses and churches closed their doors to avoid the assembly of crowds gathering in one place. The nation was under attack by an unknown virus that was attacking person to person. Hospitals were filling up. The death toll was rising to levels this generation had not known, and for the first time in my more than sixty (60) years in the ministry, we were called upon to find alternative ways to communicate God's Word to a sinful and dying people.

On a conference call with the young Mayor of the City of Montgomery, Honorable Steven Reed asked for our cooperation in making the program he was instituting successful in order to get the people well, and back to a normal life. One major problem existed: How could we help the Mayor and Governor if we could not preach to the congregation while trying to help the membership? It was the preacher's job to try to get the word to the people.

We went virtual through Social Media in order to reach our people. But as Christ commands, "Go into all the world and preach the

Introduction

gospel to every creature. He that believeth and is baptized shall be saved, but he that believeth not shall be damned." (Mark 16:15-16)

This series of sermons will touch the lost, the unbeliever, the heartbroken, the lonely, the sick, the bereaved, the faithless, and the faithful.

GOD CALLED ME: I'LL BE DAMNED IF I DON'T PREACH!!

Words In Season

"The Lord GOD hath given me the tongue of the learned, that I should know how to speak a word in season to him that is weary: he wakeneth morning by morning, he wakeneth mine ear to hear as the learned." Isaiah 50:4

✝ Words in Season

I want to talk to you this morning from a message from Isaiah, but I want to talk from the subject, "Words in Season." And let me just take you to the reading of Isaiah 50:4

"The Lord GOD hath given me the tongue of the learned, that I should should know how to speak a word in season to him that is weary: he wakeneth morning by morning, he wakeneth mine ear to hear as the learned." (KJV)

To speak words in season is a gift of God, and it's one of His best. He gives us the ability to speak suitable words in all conditions that we face. He gives us timely words in season and wise words as we try to comfort the lonely and heartbroken. And so it should encourage all Christian people to know that God has called us out to be a living witness, a living testimony to people who cry out "somebody help me!"

Have you ever been in a situation where you didn't know what to say? People were heartbroken, crying…crying out for somebody to just show you how this happened, and why this happened, and you have nothing you can say on your own? Sometimes you have to know that the season has come, that maybe it's the time that you don't say anything. I've had the occasion to encourage people along life's way for many and varied reasons, and you come to a loss for words, and you just simply sit in their presence and let them cry. And when it's all finished, the person would say to you, "thank you", and you wonder, what have I done? And then you recognize that all you had to do was listen. It is the kind of language that God has put in your life, and in your soul, that allows you to speak to situations that you don't even understand. Words can bring pleasure. In other words…words can bring good feelings. If a person whispers kind words to you, they don't even realize the good that's done in passing on that encouragement and in those encouraging words. But God gives words in a timely fashion, He gives it in season. Now, I don't mean the seasons of winter, spring, summer and fall. There are seasons in our life that come in certain places, and in certain ways, and we can't even figure out when the season arrived. You go through situations and desperations many times, and you can't figure out how you got there, or how you're going to get out. But God arranges it so, in the season of need, the season of stress. The season of loneliness, He gives you the words to speak in season. And He gives you wise words. You don't just say anything to anybody about anything. God gives you the right words to say in the season of trial and tribulation. And so He's fixed us with words in season and let us speak pleasurable words.

When you think about "Words in Season", God gives us words to speak in pain and emotional stress. We can't bear the pain or the stress of somebody on our own. What we have to do is be prepared to help them bear their pain, their burden, or their stresses in life. Say the words that God has put on your heart, that will make a significant difference.

He gives us words of joy. Words of joy can bring a smile to your face. You wonder in your life "how am I going to make it?" "How am I going to get out of this situation?" And then somebody just whispers in your ears, it's going to be alright. He brings words of joy, and a smile on your face. God also gives us words to speak not just in pain, and pleasure, and joy, but words in sorrow. Look at Jesus one day when He was on His way to Calvary to be hanged on a cross. Jesus had left the courtroom after being tried all night and then was finally found guilty and sent to the cross for crucifixion. And on His way up the hill of Calvary, a crowd had gathered. It was following Him, people were crying, and weeping, doing all of the things people do when they know somebody has been mistreated and is being mistreated. Women were crying, "don't do that, leave Him alone, He's done nothing wrong." Jesus looked at them with a cross on His shoulder, and said, *"Daughters of Jerusalem, weep not for me, but weep for yourselves and for your children. For if they do this to a green tree, what will they do in the dry?"* Words of comfort on His way to Calvary. He's speaking to people to not worry about Him, worry about your own selves, and your own children. For if they'll do it to me, what do you think they'll do to you? Let's talk about Words in Season.

Words of Cheer. These are words that are full of hope that people can literally find a way to give you hope in a hopeless situation. They can find the right words to tell you, it's going to be alright. Don't worry about it. God will fix it. God will make a way, and lighten the load on your heart and mind, and give you hope for tomorrow. He will provide you with words to speak kindly to people. You don't have to be boisterous all the time! Can't you just whisper kind words to me, so I can hear them? He gives us words to give people the bright side; talk about the positives in life. You don't have to be negative all the time. Words can give a positive outlook on what's going on right now. That when this is all over, we can recognize that God is still in charge. The bright side of life can give us words to present the positive, to bring a smile with it. Speak kind words when there is nothing but cursing and slanderous kinds of things going on. We can speak words of comfort.

He also gives us *Words of Warning*. Words of warning come from people He puts in our lives who can speak on a far sighted plane to you. Who can see the issues of our conduct? You wonder sometimes, how did that old woman, or that old man, get to be able to be so knowledgeable about life. They had lived it! They had suffered it! They had gone the last mile, and they knew enough about life to tell you, "baby that's not safe, you ought to think about what you're doing." They can help to change the conduct that you've already engaged in. He gives us *words of counsel. Words of the wise. Words of experience, and words of moral character.* You know there are people that you meet in life that you've never seen before or had contact with and somehow the attitude comes to you that, that's a person I'd like to know. They give off this air of real knowledge, experience, and life among them and around them. And I can learn from them. And so that person is in a position because God arranged it so they can share their experiences in life and provide moral character as you develop your own. A few words of reproof, brave words:

- Sometimes you need to be told no.
- Sometimes you need to be told, that's not right.
- Sometimes you need to be steered in the right direction, and let God lead you from where you are to where you ought to be. A person who can give you words of reproof can show you your thoughts, and show you that you are traveling the wrong way. And have you turn around and go on a better path.

Finally, He gives *words of comfort.* All of us need words of comfort on occasions. Somebody just show me how to make it, how to do it, how to get up from here and move on to a better way of life. And how can somebody give me words of comfort in my situation? I couldn't help but look at another scripture when I was preparing this message, and that other scripture comes from the gospel of Matthew, and I just want to read the verses that I pinpointed in giving comfort. Jesus was preaching one day and the scripture says. *"and when Jesus departed then, two blind men followed Him, crying and saying, thou Son of David, have mercy on us. And when He came into the house, the blind men came to Him, and Jesus said unto them, "believe ye, that I am able to do this?" They said unto Him, "Yea Lord." Then He touched their eyes saying "according to your faith be it unto you." (Matthew 9:27-29)* Blind men, who needed to see Jesus. They had heard about His miracles. They had heard about all of the things that He had done in their community and communities around that community. And they had that attitude that if we could just get close to Him. If He's been doing all of these things, surely, He can help us see. And Jesus went into the house, and they went in with Him. And you know how Jesus returned to them their sight? He made them understand with His words that *"your faith will make you whole."* It is the amount of faith you have that will decide" what your cure would be. And so the first thing He asked them, *do you believe I can do what you're asking me to do?" They said, "Yea, Lord."* Words in Season.

And Jesus told them, *"go seeing, your faith has made you whole."* Church, no matter what happens in life. No matter what the situation of your present day is - your faith can make you whole! Your faith can return you to the stability that you require within yourself. Every day of your life Jesus will be there to answer your faith. Somebody said, *"Faith is the substance of things hoped for, it's the evidence of things not seen."* (Hebrews 11:1)

God Bless You

God Has Made of One Blood, All Nations

"And hath made of one blood all nations of men for to dwell on all the face of the earth, and hath determined the times before appointed, and the bounds of their habitation;" Acts 17:26

✝ God Has Made of One Blood, All Nations

Let me share with you a scripture from the Acts of the Apostles, Chapter 17:22-28 (KJV):

"Then Paul stood in the midst of Mars' hill, and said, Ye men of Athens, I perceive that in all things ye are too superstitious. For as I passed by, and beheld your devotions, I found an altar with this inscription, To THE UNKNOWN GOD. Whom therefore ye ignorantly worship, him declare I unto you. God that made the world and all things therein, seeing that he is Lord of heaven and earth, dwelleth not in temples made with hands; Neither is worshiped with men's hands, as though he needed anything, seeing he giveth to all life, and breath, and all things; And hath made of one blood all nations of men for to dwell on all the face of the earth, and hath determined the times before appointed, and the bounds of their habitation; That they should seek the Lord, if haply they might feel after him, and find him, though he be not far from every one of us: For in him we live, and move, and have

our being; as certain also of your own poets have said, For we are also his offspring."

Let me talk from the topic, "God Has Made of One Blood All Nations." We've gone through some trying times of late; it's so many major things happening in our life that we don't know which one to worry most about. We've been going through a pandemic of losing health and life for the past few months over 102,000 people died in the process of awaiting for a cure. We've been unable to worship in our own house. We have been unable to meet and greet family members in these stressful times. Even worse, as you watch the news from day to day, look at the number of people who can't even find a moment to say goodbye to a loved one in the hospital. They are being moved to windows, while family members stand on the outside and say, "I love you and I want you to know this isn't a goodbye." And with all that happening in this world, at this moment with the number of people who have not only lost their lives, but families who have lost their jobs and incomes, over 40 million jobs lost, nowhere to turn, nowhere to look for help.

But we recognize that God is still on the throne. God is still in charge, and He knows what He is doing. Sometimes it's hard for us to comprehend the workings of God because it is so far out of our knowledge bank, but God is still working with the situation. In time, He will move, and we will understand it better by and by. Look at this story of Paul at Athens, Greece during Biblical times and how many things are still up for grabs. Paul, a metropolitan man, and he's in Metropolitan, Athens, Greece. Paul is a person who could adjust to any situation. He could move from town to town, village to village, and wherever God sent him he was able to make it work, not only for him but for God at that moment. And so now he is in Athens, Greece. He had just left Palestine, he had preached in Europe, one big city after another. He made this Christian tour every time somebody would call him, Paul would do his best to get there. In Athens, after answering the call of the Macedonian church after they wrote to him and asked him, "come over and help us." And now he is making that journey over to Athens to help the Macedonian church. But Paul is equipped to preach. He didn't just happen into the business. He didn't just happen one day and think, "this is a good job, I want to take this job here," God called him when he lived under another name.

The name was Saul. And he was on his way to Damascus to literally destroy the church because it believed in this Jesus Christ. And he was on his horses, and he was riding down the road, down the Damascus Road. And he said, I saw a light brighter than the sun, and I heard a voice saying to me, called me by my name, *"Saul, Saul why persecutest thou Me. Is it hard to kick against the prick?"* Saul, on that day fell off his horse to the ground, looked toward heaven and said, "Lord, what will you have me do?" And He said, I want you to go on to Damascus. I got a man who is prepared to show you what I want you to do. But now first of all, before you leave, I'm changing your name. I'm giving you the name of Paul so that you will no longer serve under the name Saul and you will carry out my mandate as you travel.

He was, as I said, a "cosmopolitan" man, he could just get along with everybody. He could find a way to make--First of all, he didn't rely on anybody to make his living for him, to give him a living, he built tents for a living as he preached the Word of God. Everywhere he went he made friends, that made friends, and they became bosom friends along the way.

But aside from being just a cosmopolitan man, he connected with people everywhere, he was fluent in the Greek language. Although he was a Jew, he came from a Jewish heritage, he was fluent in every language. For those of you who worship in the house of God know that our Bible was translated from Hebrew to Greek, and then from Greek to English. But Paul was fluent in the original language of the Greeks and he was an educated man, he could speak seven languages fluently. He was their philosopher in all things going.

But here's what he was able to prove. Not only was he well rounded and was able to preach the Word of God, he was not only fluent in the Greek language so that he could go to the Bible, and find what you're looking for, he was trained by one of the greatest minds the world had ever known. He said he was trained by Gamaliel, and that was one of the most profound thinkers of the time, at that time, and Paul was trained under him.

But now he's in Athens Greece, a cultural center that stands even today; People do business with Athens Greece today, but back then it was the cultural center of the universe. Paul walked down to see people in their normal activities of life. He saw men with great minds and abilities walking up and down in the Lyceum, at the cultural center. Every man embracing his own thoughts, and teaching his own thing, and convincing others that they ought to follow him and his God. Paul said that he watched them pace up and down in the Lyceum and ponder, and preach the most profound questions of the time. Questions of life and death and walking down the Lyceum discussing the profound thoughts of life and death- where did it come from, where is it going. All kinds of discussions about life.

They even discussed time and eternity. They recognized that time couldn't be trapped, couldn't be tamed. That time was in the hands of the unknown God. They also recognized that even God himself declared that *"time and eternity is in my hands."* Here they were going and discussing it through great length. They would talk about knowledge of feelings. It's not good enough to know something, you've got to feel something. Now, where did feelings come from? And so they discussed it as they walked and talked. They wanted to discuss what was real, and what was illusionary. How can you know the difference between what you happen to feel, and what you're feeling, and what is just a figment of your imagination?

Paul, this man as he watched Athens at the cultural center, recognized that here in Athens, Socrates had taught Plato. And Plato had taught Aristotle. And Aristotle and taught Alexander the Great, but this pauper, little man, this little Jewish tent maker, short, bald headed, a Roman citizen, a steward of Gamaliel, was preaching that Jesus Christ is the Son of God. Paul, who's moving from town to town, synagogue to synagogue; his main theme was, *I am not ashamed of the gospel. centheFor in the power of God, is salvation.* I don't want to look into my background, my knowledge, my training, the people who touch my life, I want you to know *whose* I am now. And I want you to understand that "*I'm not ashamed of the gospel. For it is the power of God unto salvation.*" (Romans 1:16)

Look at Athens one more time. Athens was full of statues, and in that area of the cultural center they had street lectures. These are the people walking up and down in the Lyceum. They had religious teachings on all religious backgrounds; each one teaching his own belief and own goal. They had intellectual groups who would stand there and tear apart a story for days upon end. They had leaders of all shapes and sizes of patriarchs, everybody had his own group, and nobody cared. Paul was there and he wanted a chance to preach Jesus on that Lyceum like everybody else. They told him he had to go to the authorities to get permission.

And Paul went to the authorities and answered them, and he said ultimately that he answered them sufficiently. While he was persuading the power structure, when all he wanted to do was teach Jesus and Him crucified, he said that they gave him permission to speak on Mars Hill, and he went out to preach one God. God is the Lord of the Universe. God is the beginning of all things. God is the creator of the Universe. God made us in His likeness, and into us He blew the breath of life. God did all of these things for us, and I want you to understand He does not live in the temples.

Well where does God live? He's not housed in a cloud in space, and you got to find Him when you find time to find Him. God is everywhere at the same time. He lives in the heart of man. Wherever you are, God is. He doesn't need temples. He doesn't need idols. He don't need nothing. *He made of one blood, all men*! Makes no difference where you come from and what color your skin, God gave us all one blood. We're still kin to everybody we come in contact with. It's time for this world to understand that you can't change that. You have to accept that God is the author and finisher of everything. It makes no difference where you live, and what town you came from, what job you have, how much stuff you've got. God gave us one blood.

I'm gone quit now. God has no favorites. If you notice as you read scripture God, makes no difference in us when it comes to blessings. If God was like some of us, He would make the sun shine on the other side of the street and leave you in the dark. Or when your crop is bitter from the heat keeping the rain away from your farm. God's not like that. God takes care of all of us, and none of us is abandoned. Jesus said one day, you must be born again. *"Except you become as a little child, you cannot enter the Kingdom of Heaven."* (Matthew 18:3)

And so, how you gonna continue to believe that God got only the east side of heaven your stuff, and on the west side is my stuff. No, no, no, God has no favorites. We are all His children. Wherever we come from, who we are, we are God's children. He loves us all. Every one of us, and He knows all about us. He knows our faults and our failures. All of us need salvation. He sent Jesus Christ, His Son, to die for us, to be raised for all of us, and to be ascended to Heaven on behalf of all of us. God does not, doesn't have favorites. Jesus died on the cross not because He was little but because He was powerful. While He was on that cross, His prayer was, Father forgive them, for they know not what they do. And He went on to heaven, came back as He said, I'll rise on the third day. And He rose declaring *"all power, in Heaven and in Earth , is in My hand."* God will not make differences in His children. He loves us all. He brought us all into the world. He'll take care of us. He knows what's going on. Sometimes we have to suffer as we use one of the blessings that God has granted us.

God Has Made of One Blood, All Nations

We are made of one blood-all men. Have you ever noticed how desperate the world becomes for somebody else's blood sometimes? Doctors are crying out, I need this blood type. I need somebody to donate some blood. What you need blood for? I've got to give it to another person. So your blood is good for another person. And another person's blood is good for you. God made all men of one blood.

God Bless You

When God Seems Distant

"And I will wait upon the Lord, that hideth his face from the house of Jacob, and I will look for him." Isaiah 8:17 (KJV)

✝ When God Seems Distant

In the book of Isaiah, Chapter 8, verses 13-17, it reads:

"Sanctify the Lord of hosts himself; and let him be your fear, and let him be your dread. And he shall be for a sanctuary; but for a stone of stumbling and for a rock of offence to both the houses of Israel, for a gin and for a snare to the inhabitants of Jerusalem. And many among them shall stumble, and fall, and be broken, and be snared, and be taken. Bind up the testimony, seal the law among my disciples. And I will wait upon the Lord, that hideth his face from the house of Jacob, and I will look for him." (KJV)

For the next few minutes, I want to talk to you about "When God seems Distant." We go through these trying times of not knowing, not being able to find answers to perplexing problems, and being charged with the responsibility of living at a distance from each other, living basically to ourselves. Many times in a very lonely position; wondering what the end will bring and where do we go from here? In the midst of it all, it seems that God is far off, that He is not listening to our prayers; that God is at a distance. But I want you to know today that despite the anguish of our times, you need to know and remember that God is real, that God has not left us alone. He's not giving us up to satan. We may be tested and tried, but God is there, sitting out in the midst at a time when we can come to grips with ourselves.

It's easy to worship God when everything is fine. You got food in your cupboard because you've been out shopping to get you six weeks or more stock in your cabinets! You don't have to worry about food at the moment. It's easy to worship God when we know we've got friends and our friends have not left us. Even though they can't stand beside us, they tell us on a regular basis, "I'm still your friend." It's easy to worship God when family is intact…when loved ones that are born, the next of kin are there, helping and encouraging you every step of the way. It's easy to worship God when your health is good. No pain, no struggle, no diseases that you don't know anything about, and you are able to walk on your own two feet. You are able to go about your business from day to day, no matter what crisis you may face, it's easy to thank God for health.

It's easy to worship God when there is happiness in your heart, and there are those who can make you smile, and make you laugh from day to day. Circumstances are not always pleasant, but when we come to a moment or circumstance beyond our control, we're reminded that it's

harder to praise God. We wonder, "Has He left me?" "Why don't you come and see about me?"

What do you do when God seems distant? You can depend on your friends, you can depend on your family, you can depend on all of those you've got around you whenever you call them, you can depend on them. But somehow it seems God has placed Himself at a distance, and we don't know what the future holds, or what tomorrow will bring.

The deepest level of worship, and you need to remember this — the deepest level of worship is praising God in a state of panic. When life is challenging you, and the body seems to be quitting on you, you've got to know that you can cry out to God and say, "Help me Lord," and He will. So, the deepest level is thanking God and praising God during your trials.

The deepest level of worship is also trusting Him when you are tempted. Surrendering while you are suffering and loving Him when He seems far away. People know when God seems distant, you may think God is angry with you. God is not angry with you. You may think God is disciplining you for some sin that you have not accounted for, but when God seems distant, I can assure you that you can rest upon the point- that God is testing your faith. *"Faith is the substance of things hoped for, it's the evidence of things not seen."* (Hebrews 11:1) So when God seems distant, He's testing your faith. We will all be tested.

Job complained, *"I go east, but He's not there. I turn and go west, but I cannot find Him. If I go North, He is hidden. When I finally go south, I cannot find Him. But I know, He knows where I am. And when He's finished testing me; I am fully certain that I will come out as pure gold."*

Tell God how you feel. Pour your heart out. Unload every emotion to Him. Job said, *"I can't be quiet, I'm angry and bitter, I have to speak."* He cried out when God seemed distant.

God can handle your doubts, your anger, your fears, your grief. Confess to Him, and God will provide relief to your ills and your pain. Remember what God has already done. Think of what Jesus went through. He never committed a sin, He never did anything wrong to anybody, helped everybody along the way and yet He ended up on Calvary, hung on a cross dying for man's sin and crying, *"Father, forgive them for they know not what they do."* Think and remember what God has done for you physically, mentally, and spiritually. The separation from God put a weight on Jesus just for a moment, and He cried out in the darkness of His hour, *"My God, My God, why hast Thou forsaken me?"* But then the light broke, the sun came up, and everybody recognized that God answered the call of Jesus Christ, and told Him to come on home, and Jesus said, *"Into Thy hands I commend my Spirit."* He gave up everything, so that He could get everything.

Jesus gave up life, so that He could gain your life and mine. I accept being abused and misused, so that He could wash away the abuse that is levied on us.

And so as I bring this message to an end; you need to understand when God seems distant, He's not gone, He's not away, He hasn't left you alone, God is just checking your faith, and your faith will make you whole.

God Bless You, and God Keep You

The Anchor of the Soul

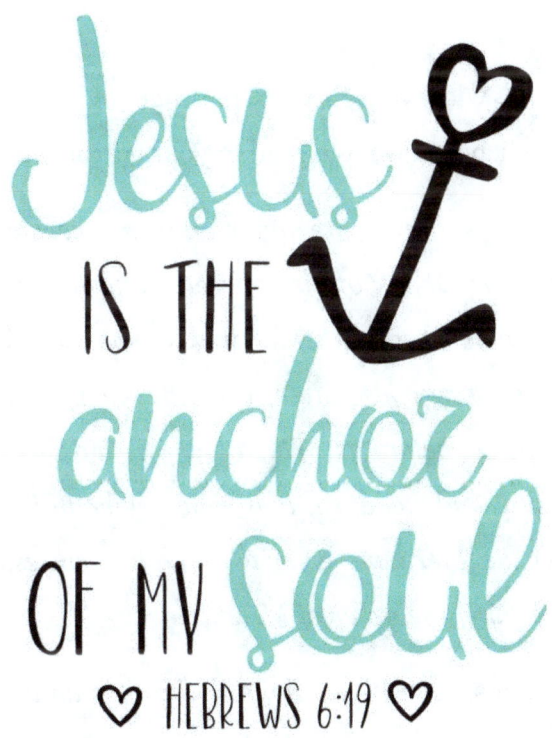

"Which hope we have as an anchor of the soul, both sure and stedfast, and which entereth into that within the veil;" Hebrews 6:19

† The Anchor of The Soul

Let me share with you for the message today from the book of Hebrews 6th chapter, I want to read in your hearing verses 17 - 20:

"Wherein God, willing more abundantly to shew unto the heirs of promise the immutability of his counsel, confirmed it by an oath: That by two immutable things, in which it was impossible for God to lie, we might have a strong consolation, who have fled for refuge to lay hold upon the hope set before us: Which hope we have as an anchor of the soul, both sure and steadfast, and which entereth into that within the veil Whither the forerunner is for us entered, even Jesus, made an high priest forever after the order of Melchisedec.

Verse 19 again says, *" Which hope we have as an anchor of the soul, both sure and steadfast, and which entereth into that within the veil;"* With that scripture I want to talk a few minutes about, *" The Anchor of the Soul."* That word immutability may be new or rather strange to some people who have not read the scripture often. But what it simply means is these are divine attributes of unchangeableness in God. God is eternally the same. He's the same in essence, in mold and direction.

The text suggests that the Christian life is a life of storms; and all of us present today can attest to a lot of storms in our lives. That many times you can't even predict them, as sometimes they rise up out of nowhere, but you have to be prepared to weather the storms of life, and you must recognize that the God we serve is able to deliver you through the storms that rage all around you.

Look at some of the storms we have. The storm of persecution. We have gone through several days and weeks now of protests and struggle to come out on the right side of life's struggles. The storm of persecution rages with us all the time. You don't want to just think that persecution is when somebody just beat you up. Look at the ways we can be persecuted on a daily basis. We can be persecuted by hunger. Not even having food to eat nor being able to work and make a living enough to buy the food we need. Persecution can be placing us on the wrong side of history and making it appear that we are nothing more than animals or strangers in a strange land.

Persecution can be not being able to buy a home for a family to live in, because there is not enough territory left in the neighborhood for us to have a place to live in. Persecution can be when somebody treats you like you are a non- person. Makes no difference who you are, where you've been, what you got, and all this other stuff, you can still be persecuted in a land of plenty, and cause the world to believe that we are nothing but beggars in a strange land. It's a storm raging around us.

It's a storm raging when we cannot find enough employment to go to work where we want to work, and to do what we know and understand is the best thing for us to do. Somehow we're skipped over all the graces of life, and all the things we should have ordinarily just because we are God's children.

Then there's the storm of doubt. There are times in your life when no matter how much, how many thoughts you have that you can survive anything doubt creep up on you, make you feel that you're not worthy of getting where you ought to be and where you're trying to be and so you're doubtful that you have the strength, the power and the knowledge to get to where you need to go.

There's a storm of inward corruption. satan is always after our soul, and no matter how we attempt to trust in God, satan can sneak in and leave doubts in our mindset and make us believe that he has another, and a better way for us to get to where we ought to be. One day after Job had given up his life to God he had become a renowned person in the community of men. He had power, he had wealth. He had a good Christian family that he had raised by the word of God. One day satan walked up to God. God asked him, what are you doing? satan says, I'm just coming from up and down the land trying to see what I can devour. And God bragged on Job and said, have you considered my servant Job? That he's righteous in all of his ways. satan said yes, I've considered Job. I've considered him often. I know he's no different from any other man, if you let me get my hands on him. And so, if you will just do one thing, and I'll show you, what the book of Job says, "if you'll just take the hedge from around him- the hedge of protection, the hedge of your loving care, you just remove the hedge, and I'll make Job curse you to your face." The Lord said, "I'll take a chance at that; you take whatever you want from Job, but you leave his life alone." When this test is all over. When the storm of interruption had subsided, Job declared, The Lord giveth, and the Lord has taken away, blessed be the name of the Lord. Of all my appointed time, I will wait until my change comes."

Then you have storms of adversity. I don't care how hard you work at success, and try to get to where you want to go, something is always tugging at you, pulling you back, and knocking you down. Storm raging. While a storm is raging on the inside, other storms rage on the outside. When all the storms have tested you, there is one storm left to take you.

But blessed be to God, the Christian possesses complete security in the midst of the storms. Church, we may have our troubles now in days present, in days to come, days past, but one thing we can recognize is that God is in charge of our life, our destiny, wherever we go from here, and how do we get there? He's complete security in the midst of the storms.

Christian's hope is in our God. Of the three great abiding graces, Faith, Hope & Love. Hope is the one that receives the least confidence in our thoughts. We have faith. We hold on to our faith, and we try to love according to the love that Jesus taught us. But somewhere sandwiched all in between faith and hope is love. Sometimes hope is squeezed between faith and love, and we have to go back and figure out what we want to do with hope. Hope is the one that receives the least confidence. Faith is the root, love is the full grown flower, but Hope occupies that intermediate position. Hope is just one of the first developments of faith. Hope is a sprout from the root of faith. Hope has the blessed foundation. It soothes between faith and love. Sometimes hope will need to come in and soothe your upsets. When your faith gets weak, love will abide. Hope comes and says, hold on just a little while longer. Hope calms fears and apprehension. We remember faith and love, but every now and then fear takes over, and apprehensions come. Paul said, "I count not myself to have apprehended but this one thing I do; in forgetting those things which are behind me, looking forward to those things which are before, I press toward the mark of the high calling in Jesus."

So hope cheers our minds in the midst of the storm. There was a story told about an ancient seaman. The seaman hauled the strongest anchor on the ship that they sailed as the safest anchor, and designed to be the last hope for times when the ship was in real danger. Every ship must have an anchor. You got to be able to set down in stormy seas near when the waves keep rocking and rolling, the anchor must be strong enough to go down not just in the depths of the water, but it must be able to go down into the ground underneath the water, and it must hold to the point that the ship cannot be moved. And so that strong anchor cannot afford brake, or drag. It must be firmly on the ground; No wind storm should be able to break her, and breach its hold on the ship, and on the ground.

Let me just say this: That anchor must be out of the reach of destruction and damage, and even the depth of death. We got an anchor in Jesus. Jesus knows our struggles. He knows how greatly we have suffered, and how we almost went down to the ground. But isn't it amazing how God can take the storms, and just push em around you, and let you stand on solid ground. Or He can take the storm, and move it in another direction.

God is in Jesus, our anchor. Christ our Savior is not only for us in the Heavens, our hope follows Him there. When I read this business of, Jesus is the anchor of the soul, I could understand what the poet was writing when he wrote the words, "O, I Want to See Him, to look upon His face; There to sing forever of His saving Grace. On the streets of Glory, let me lift my voice; Cares all past, home at last, ever to rejoice."

When you have been attaching yourself to the anchor of Jesus Christ, who is our Savior in all the trials and the storms we have. He can pull us even out of the reach of death. He did that! He knows what we need in troubled times, and in storms of life. He's the Son of God, He knows our troubles. He is our anchor! Yes, every ship needs an anchor. Every soul needs an anchor. When I compare the destiny of a ship, the life of people on a ship on deep waters, how the waters can rage and carry on overnight. You wake up the next morning, You're been tossed and turned; Sometimes all you need to do is just hope that you can reach the ground, and then you're depending on the anchor of that ship to attach itself to the ground.

In life, the Christian only hopes that when the day comes, the night is now past, the anchor in Jesus holds us in time of storms and He is the Son of God, and He knows our troubles. Church, in times like these we need a Savior. In times like these we need an anchor. Be very sure, be very sure, your anchor holds and grips the solid rock. This rock is Jesus. He's the one. This rock is Jesus- the only one. So be sure, be very sure, your anchor holds and grips the solid rock.

God Bless You

Life's Eraser

"And looking round about upon them all, he said unto the man, Stretch forth thy hand. And he did so: and his hand was restored whole as the other." Luke 6:10

✝ Life's Eraser

I want to share with you a scripture from the gospel of Luke, 6th chapter, and I want to read in your hearing verses 6-12, and then share a message from there:

"And it came to pass also on another sabbath, that he entered into the synagogue and taught: and there was a man whose right hand was withered. And the scribes and Pharisees watched him, whether he would heal on the sabbath day; that they might find an accusation against him. But he knew their thoughts, and said to the man which had the withered hand, Rise up, and stand forth in the midst. And he arose and stood forth. Then said Jesus unto them, I will ask you one thing; Is it lawful on the sabbath days to do good, or to do evil? to save life, or to destroy it? And looking round about upon them all, he said unto the man, Stretch forth thy hand. And he did so: and his hand was restored whole as the other. And they were filled with madness;

and communed one with another what they might do to Jesus. And it came to pass in those days, that he went out into a mountain to pray, and continued all night in prayer to God. (KJV)

I want to share with you a message that I delivered some years ago for the first time, and I took the subject of that message from the comics in the newspaper. I always loved to read *Dennis the Menace,* cause he's always in something, and his mother's always calling his attention to come out of whatever he's doing, and settle down and be good. So on this particular day, Dennis had gotten in trouble and his mother punished him, and sent him to the corner of the room to sit and face the wall, and stay there until she told him to come out. And while he was sitting there, Dennis said, *"I wish life came with an eraser."* Think about it. That was a good point. If he could just erase the problems he got in, he wouldn't have all that pressure, and so I think he represents so many of us today, in our present lives that we make so many blunders, so many mistakes, we do things that violate those that love us; even our own selves. Sometimes in our thoughts and mind, we disappoint our own selves, and we wish out loud, if my mistakes could just be erased.

Jesus knew that. Jesus knew that we are prone to error, to sin and all kinds of violations of truth and trust. Some that we commit deliberately,
and others just by accident but the result is the same. We just wish somehow, whatever we have done, could just be erased, and you never

have to think about it again, or be bothered with that situation. Jesus went to the temple, and He had already gotten Himself with the population of people who distrusted Him with being so powerful, and connected so well with God and with the Heavenly Host that they felt it had to be some way that they could bring Him down and stop Him from using the power that God had given Him. But in that particular room that day, not only was Jesus Christ the Son of God present, but Jesus the eraser was there.

This man that came into notice was a man with a withered hand. His right hand had lost its strength, and he had not the ability to use the most powerful place on his body-his right hand, the place of power in that body. He noticed that daily he was losing strength, that it started out with just a pain and kept moving downward until finally it was going so he couldn't even use his hand. And he discovered that the longer it lasted, the older he got, the more he lost his strength in that hand, until finally all of his strength was gone.

Jesus had healed several people prior to healing this man. He had been known as a healer, and the community was watching Him to see what violation He could do or create as He moved about the community doing good. And the one thing they felt they could get Him on is that the Ten Commandments had told us to, *"Remember the Sabbath day to keep it holy."* And that no man was to do any work on the Sabbath day.

We were supposed to do all our work in six days, but on the Sabbath day, it was a day of rest. And here Jesus is healing people as He goes by; it made no difference about the day of the week. What concerned Him was the condition of a person, and whenever somebody called out for help, in whatever situation they were in, Jesus took the time to heal them. And they watched it. I remember when we went into the services of the cross on Easter Sunday there was a scripture that says, sitting down, they watched Him there." And these people were doing just that, on this day, sitting down watching Him to see what He would violate in their rules of order, and law And Jesus walked into this place on the Sabbath- "entered into the synagogue and taught: and there was a man whose right hand was withered. And the scribes and Pharisees watched Him, whether he would heal on the Sabbath day; that they might find an accusation against him."

Look at what Jesus did in this brazen act. He looked at that man with that withered hand and said, rise up. And of course the man jumped up, because he had been doubtful about Jesus too, and he knew the possibilities of something happening to him in a real way, and so he didn't even question whether he knew about the law. He stood up at Jesus' request. And when he stood up, Jesus said, *"I'll ask you one thing. Is it lawful on the Sabbath Day to do good?, or to do evil?, to save life?, or to destroy it?"* And then He said to the man, *"Stretch out your hand."* Now come on! Here is a man whose hand is withered, all the strength is gone. He's had no use of his right hand for years now, and here this Jesus is saying, "Stand up, and raise your right hand," and his hand was made whole.

Christ was in the right place at the right time. There was a man who needed help there, and Christ was there, think about it. Whatever your needs are, wherever you are, you just be in the presence of Jesus Christ, and Christ is there to heal you, and to bless you in any way necessary. Christ had the privilege for good, and He wasn't about to let this crowd at the synagogue stop Him from doing what God had sent Him to do.

The man came with his right hand withered. He was powerless. He had gradually lost his strength day by day, his strength just disappeared. Now it's completely gone. He can't work with it. He can't make his mark in society because his right hand is his power hand, and it's gone. So, he's become a helpless creature with a withered hand- he couldn't make his mark in the world.

As I look at this situation. He's sitting in the corner, wishing he just had an eraser. The man is sitting in the corner of the synagogue wishing he could just get a little help with his right hand, and Jesus is there. That's the action of sin. Sin is a disabling spiritual disease. It slowly wears us down. Sin operates in a strange way. You can be hard at work trying to be good and decent, and right, and helpful in society, and satan just comes to start creeping in your life to make you something different from what you've been praying to be, and it becomes a disabling effect.

Sin will make you turn away from worship. I realize we got a problem right now in terms of distancing we have to keep in order to worship together. But you know, this didn't just happen, it's been eating at us a long time. And so we have a disabling spiritual disease that has started to prevent us from worshiping God because we had doubts that He exists. It makes us not recognize, and rejoice in the faith. We want to go and do something entirely different. Sin will make you not even delight in knowing God. You can't be obedient to His plans, and it will even affect your chance of developing the same character that you find in Jesus Christ.

But Christ came to fix that. Christ came to restore us as whole again as people of faith, and people who understand that God is real. Jesus came to erase our sins away. He said you must be born again. But being born again is accepting Christ as your eraser- that whatever sins you've committed, whatever problems you face along life's way, and giving yourself the wrong orders, Jesus came to fix it. And so He erases our sins away. So He said to this man, *"Stretch forth thy hand."* Here's a sick man, a withered arm, not able to pick up anything, not even his arm. And Jesus said to him, *"raise your hand."*, and he raised it. Christ came to provide us a healing of mind, body and spirit, and He will do it for all of us on any given day. He came to show us our true selves. Jesus came to show us who we are, and He also came to show us what we can be. When we look at ourselves in the light of Jesus Christ, and what He has done for human suffering we recognize that we have failed in such ways, that we need Him to guide us, to protect us, to cleanse us.

And so, He came to let us know who we are. We are sinners. We are lost. We're down in the dust, in the dungeon. But He came also to show us what He can do. He can take our sins away, and make us as He is. He is the Christ, the Son of God, and He's given us a place in God's Kingdom.

Finally, Christ is this eraser you cried out for. Christ is the eraser that erased the withered man's disease from him. And Christ is my eraser. He erase away my sins, and take away my iniquities. Christ erases not only my sin, but my faults- whatever problems I have, He looks beyond my faults and sees my need! And that's why I'll see Him as my eraser!

He knows my failures. There are times when I have failed most miserably. I have Him down, me down, and everybody that loves me down. But Jesus Christ is my eraser, and He will erase all of my iniquities, my doubts, and my fears.

So church, Dennis had a good point. He gets punished in life so often. And if he could just have an eraser, to erase it away, he could be better off under the circumstances. And life for us is that way. Every day we sin, every day we have faults, every day we have failures, every day! But, Jesus came to erase it away, and that's the Jesus we serve. Jesus is our eraser.

God Bless You

The Benefits of Being in God's Family

"Beloved, now are we the sons of God, and it doth not yet appear what we shall be: but we know that, when he shall appear, we shall be like him; for we shall see him as he is." 1 John 3:2

† The Benefits of Being in God's Family

For the benefit of those of you who are listening to the service today wherever you are. I want to put in perspective something that we had to skip on Friday which was Good Friday, and ordinarily we would worship by presenting the seven last words of Jesus on the cross. We are all victims of the tragic health problem in this nation, and we can't do things as we normally would on any given day, but we can do the best we can to represent our Lord and Savior Jesus Christ. It's about Him. It's about the sacrifice He made for us. The life He gave, that we may have life. So what I'd like to do before I start the message is just kind of review what we would have done on Friday as we celebrated the seven last words of Jesus on the cross.

Luke tells us in Luke 23, that when Jesus was hung on the cross nails had been put in His hands and His feet, and He was bleeding and dying. But instead of Jesus complaining about what the enemy had done to Him, His first words from the cross was a prayer. His prayer was for the whole world. His prayer was, Father, forgive them for they know not what they do.

And the next word that He uttered also comes from Luke 23 when one of the male factors who were hanged beside Him, one on the right and one on the left, for crimes they had committed, and Jesus was hanging there on the center cross, and the whole community knew that He had done no wrong. He was not guilty of what they were accusing Him of. One male factor said to Him, "If you be the Christ, why don't you save yourself and us and come down off the cross." The other male factor said to him, said to the one who had just cried out why don't you save us. He said, "You ought to be ashamed of yourself. We are here because we have been guilty of what they accuse us of. We have done wrong. We have murdered, stolen, betrayed trust. But this man has done nothing wrong." Nothing amiss. And then he looked into the face of Jesus and said to Him, "Master, when Thou comest into Thy Kingdom, remember me." Jesus didn't think about it. He just simply said to him, *"Verily, I say unto thee, Today, Thou shalt be with Me in Paradise."*

And it took care of not only the world's problem; He answered the cry of an individual who needed His help. Even while He was dying.
And then His mother was crying at His grave, at His cross, at the feet of Jesus. She was weeping tears because of her child, her firstborn child, was being hanged on that cross. Nothing she could do about it to

stop what was going on, and Jesus looked down upon His mother as John would tell us about it in John 19:26 and say he said, *"Woman, behold thy son, son behold thy mother."* In other words, He took the time to see about His mother before leaving this world, and put her in the hands of another disciple of His, and said to him, '*behold thy mother,"* and said to His mother, " *behold thy son, go home with him."* and she lived with John until her death.

And then Jesus at that point on the cross had finished doing what He came to do for the world. *"Father forgive them, for they know not what they do."* He'd already done for an individual what He came to do in the crisis moment of his life. He cried out, Father, when Thy come into Thy Kingdom, remember me." And Jesus said, *"Today, thou shalt be with me in paradise."* And then, He took time to see about family matters, and take care of His mother before He died.

And then He looked up to Heaven, and reconnected with the Father, and said, *"My God, my God, why hast Thou forsaken me?"*
Matthew 27 teaches us that. He knew God had sent Him, He just had to reconnect with the Father. And then when He finished that He said, *"I thirst".* The body bled, the liquids in His body were going out. There was nothing to refresh Him as He died on the cross. And so He cried, *"I thirst."* Somebody decided to give Him some vinegar and gall. Jesus said after that moment, *"It is finished."* John tells us in 19: 30 Jesus said, *"It is finished."* What I came for. What you sent me for, I have done, and it is finished. And He looked up to heaven one

last time and said, *"Father into Thy hands I commend My Spirit."* And gave up the ghost.

But just for a moment, I want to take you back to what He said to the soul that said, "Lord, when you come into your Kingdom, please remember me." And Jesus said to him, "Today, thou shalt be with me in paradise." Look at what I John says in scripture, 3:1-3:

"Behold, what manner of love the Father hath bestowed upon us, that we should be called the sons of God: therefore the world knoweth us not, because it knew him not. Beloved, now are we the sons of God, and it doth not yet appear what we shall be: but we know that, when he shall appear, we shall be like him; for we shall see him as he is." And every man that hath this hope in him purifieth himself, even as he is pure." (KJV)

Let me talk for just a few minutes about, *"The Benefits of Being in God's Family."* When we place our faith in Christ, God becomes our father, we become His children, other believers become our brothers and sisters, the church becomes our spiritual family. The family of the past, the present, and the future. When you accept Jesus Christ as your Savior, you have now entered the family of God. God is now your father. You have become His child. We are His children, and He often said in His scriptural references, *"suffer little children to come unto me. Forbid them not, for such is the Kingdom of heaven."* All the people who believe, who trust in Jesus Christ, I don't care what their color, what race they may have come from, if they believe in Jesus Christ, they have now become your sisters and brothers, for we all belong to Him and God is our father.

Look at the earthly family that God constructed. We all come from one. We have kinfolks, we have brothers and sisters, who were born the next of kin. But as we travel through this world, we recognize that family is what is considered the primary family. That one will fade away. Look at the wonderful gift from God, in giving us family ties. The one thing we must recognize, that no matter how much we love and care for each other as we were born the next of kin; this family is only temporary. It can only last a while. Moses prayed one day in the 90th number of Psalms and said, "*if we live seventy years, four score years and ten, three score years and ten, seventy but, if we lived four score years it was nothing but labor and sorrow, soon cut off, and we fly away.*"

And so, life is only temporary here on this earth, and it's fragile. Look at the number of things that go wrong in the run of a day, in a week, in a month, in a year. Last year we weren't even thinking about a virus hitting this country, and destroying so many people that we loved and cared for. It's even touched us in ways we can't even explain. It's fragile. We are like glass, we break. We give up so many things in our lives that we cannot regain, regain or re-capture. But we cherish the fact that we have that chance. Some families are broken by divorce, the love thing. Nobody cares anymore. And so we find ourselves separated from each other, traveling long distances and can't even keep in touch.

I was thinking just the other day when I heard a person had passed away in a state that we know very well, and it only had two people left in the family; two sisters. The one sister living in California, another sister living in Mississippi. And too far, too old, and too sick to even make this funeral. We're fragile. We're broken by distance. We think we're young and we can take the world. We can travel wherever we want, and get back whenever we choose. But the distance, many times, keeps us away from each other, and then old age will take control. We can't do anything about it, we just sit there each day in age, time and circumstance. And then finally, when we are finished growing old, death separates us, comes and gets us.

Our spiritual family, though, will continue through eternity. Let me share with you what God gave us as a family here on this earth. What God gave us was a family name. None of us have anything to do with our mothers and fathers, who they were, how they got to be. That was something God that had control of. You had nothing to do with it. He gave you a family likeness. We grow up, and we grow old just like the person who bore us.

We are genetically made up. We are the same blood. One way or the other we become as parents in this world. He gave us family privileges. Some of us survive it, and some don't. Then He gave us family intimate access. Some people have keys to the house, others don't. Some people have keys to the heart, others don't. But He gave us the privilege to have access. And then we have the family inheritance. Whatever is left somehow belongs to us, if we have lived the kind of life that satisfies the giver. But I want to finish this. I want to look at what God has given in return for what we've lost.

Look at the riches of His grace. Somebody wrote a song one time that says, *"Grace woke me up this morning. Grace started me on my way. Grace will make me love all of my enemies. Grace will brighten up my day."* God delivered us Grace, and with it kindness. Look at those we've come to know and come to love who give us acts of kindness beyond measure. Many times they don't know us, never met us, have no way of determining where you came from or where you're going. But out of the kindness of their hearts, they do what is right and pleasing in God's sight to help you in need.

God gave us patience. He taught us how to wait. Wait on Him, wait on His change, because change will come. *"They that wait on the Lord shall renew their strength, they shall mount up with wings as eagles, run and not be weary, walk and not faint."* (Isaiah 40:31) God gave us Glory. Glory, glory to His name. God gave us wisdom. He gave us a chance to know, and to understand how to rightly divide the word of truth. God gave us power, and mercy. When we have sinned, and come short of the glory of God, He will have mercy upon us, give us His lovingkindness.

Finally, what are my benefits in this: One of the benefits of my loving Jesus Christ, and becoming a part of the Christian family, and being God's child, is that He will give me a new home. See, earth is not my home; I said, it's just temporary, it's just for a while. But Jesus said before He went to Calvary, *"In My Father's house are many mansions. If it were not so, I would have told you. I go to prepare a place for you, that where I am, there ye may be also."* (John 14:2)

So, He's got a new home over in Glory. He will completely change us to be like Christ. And you know that's something to do. For God to be willing and able to change us from this creature that we are to the person, and creature we ought to be is a feat in itself. Free from pain. This epidemic of health failure will end. It will pass. Christ says, I go to prepare a place for you, and I'm going to suffer pain to do it. So that eventually you will have no pain, no suffering and death. It will be no more. No more crying, no more dying. We thank Christ Jesus for doing that on our behalf, and we know that there will be no more pain.

God Bless You

Fainting In The Day of Adversity

"If thou faint in the day of adversity, thy strength is small."
Proverbs 24:10

✝ Fainting In The Day of Adversity

Let me explain what I'm attempting to do with the messages I'm preparing under these adverse circumstances that we exist and live under today. I thought because we're distant from each other, we have so many of our people who cannot attend church services as they normally would and people are scattered all over the city and state and other states as well. I want you to know that what I am doing is preparing messages that will speak to the problems we face and to somehow invite you to look at God's solution to the problems we face.

A couple of Sundays ago we started the outreach program I talked about, "When God Seems Distant", and tried to show you that God is really here, we just feel that way sometimes. And last Sunday I took a message from the seven last words of Jesus on the cross. When one of the men who was hanging beside Him asked Him, *"Master, when Thou cometh into Thy Kingdom, remember me."* And Jesus without hesitation said to him, *"Today thou shalt be with me in paradise."* And I tried to show how God in Jesus was taking care of business on His way out of this world.

Fainting In The Day of Adversity

Today, I want to take you to Proverbs Chapter 24 verse 10. And just that one verse I want to read for you, and feel free when you take your Bible to go and read it again. That 10th verse says:

"If thou faint in the day of adversity, thy strength is small." (KJV)

And so let me just talk a few minutes about fainting in the day of adversity. You know we can't help but think about what's happening to us in this world of ours. We can't understand, we can't seem to stop it in its tracks. People are getting sick and dying all over this world, not just a state or city but all over this world, and we are caught up in this strange scene where normally we believe that we could be in charge of what is going on around us, but we find ourselves in a situation where we are helpless. Strength is tested by the day of adversity.

The day of adversity will come no matter who we are, where you are, what you do in life, how successful you've been at doing what you do. We've got to know that the day of adversity will come. The dark day of adversity will rise on every soul of man. You know it makes no difference about your standing in life, your position, your wealth, or all of the things you've accumulated in this world. It makes no difference. The day of adversity will rise on every one of us; sooner or later. It cannot be eluded whether it's in your youth, whether it's with your good health or whether you have what you think is strength of body.

Look at the number of people who felt well and became sick. Look at the number of people who thought they had everything together and then one day they couldn't hardly breathe. Look at the people who go out and lift weights all day long, and have a good body, physique just builds their bodies in strength of what they would like to see in the end, and then one day strength is gone. Strength is wanted for the day of adversity. This is a truth and true of sorts when life is attacked by all kinds of crises, problems, burdens, diseases, illnesses, and you cannot understand. The day of adversity will assault us in ways that we can't fight back. Nobody can help us. We feel that we must give up.

Here we are in these trying times, the strength that we had will find ourselves in a strain many times. The burden, the load is too heavy for the body to bear. When adversity comes, we can't pick up the load we thought we could pick up. We can't carry it up the hill, we can't even carry it down the hill. The strain will take control of our body, and our strength. Pressures will get all over us. All of us, each day, whether we are alone or partly separated; we find ourselves under the pressure of the weight of the load of the burden we carry. "Lord, I don't know what's going to happen to me, give me health and strength." You say, Lord, lift them up from this position I am in. Pick me up, and prop me on the leaning sides that keep me going towards the ground. The pressures will get on us, all over us, and we won't be able to handle them on our own.

The soul is diseased with the danger of being crushed. Sometimes you look at your relationship with Jesus Christ, and you know He's been with you all of this time. He's kept you from falling, He's propped you on leaning sides, He's given you what you needed and then all of a sudden it seems like as I said in an earlier sermon He's distant, He walked away, and you can't seem to get Him back with you.

There's a need for sufficient strength. You see, a lighthouse must not only be strong enough to stand in the calm weather, it must be able to resist the battering ram of the tempest. I look sometimes at the welcome sign in the harbor of New York where the statue stands and welcomes people from all over the world as they come into the Harbor; makes no difference where you come from as long as you're entering the Harbor of New York; you'll see her with raised hands- "give me your tired, your poor," and they're coming into a country that they felt it was much easier to survive, much better to live in. But that statue has stood the test of time. It stood in good weather, and stood in bad, and she still stands with outstretched arms, welcoming people from yonders world.

No, a ship cannot be built for calm waters. I sailed the Pacific Ocean, and there were times when the waters were so calm, you could forget that you were floating on deep waters. And then there were other times when the storms would rise, and the waves would grow, and the ship was tossed from one side to the other. And it seemed like it wouldn't survive. That means a ship cannot just be built for calm waters, it must be built for the storm.

A lamp is useless if it goes out in darkness. You don't need a lamp in the light, you need a lamp in the darkness. So a lamp is no good to you if it goes out in the darkness. My Christian friends, brothers and sisters let me tell you this; religion is for times of trial and temptations. The spiritual light needs to be strong. Strong enough to hold on through trials and terror, and temptation & trouble. Get your strength, build it in Jesus. But you've got to have faith. Faith and courage will give strength in the day of adversity. When these trials come, when troubles get in your way, faith will keep you strong-and keep you working against the tide. Faith is the substance of things hoped for, it's the evidence of things not seen. The secret of the highest courage is faith. If you will have courage, if you will be strong in the process of all that is going on, then you must have faith. He who trusts God is armed with mighty armor. If you trust God, when your strength fails, God will pick you up. If you trust God when it seems like everything is going wrong, He can make it right. And you need to put your faith in God. The scripture tells us that even the youth shall faint and be weary. The young shall ultimately fall, but they that wait upon the Lord shall renew their strength. *"They shall mount up with wings eagles, run and not be weary; they shall walk and not faint."* (Isaiah 40:31) Don't faint, God will take care of you.

There's a song I like so well that says, '*God Will Take Care of You: be not dismayed, whatever betide, God will take of you; beneath his wings of love abide, God will take care of you. No matter what may be the test, God will take care of you. Lean weary one upon His breast, God will take care of you. God will take care of you through every day, all the way, He will take care of you. God will take care of you.'*

God Bless You

Small Things

"Shall we give, or shall we not give? But he, knowing their hypocrisy, said unto them, Why tempt ye me? bring me a penny, that I may see it." Mark 12:15

Small Things

I want to call your attention to the gospel of Saint Mark. In the New Testament we have the four gospels, Matthew, Mark, Luke and John. And I want to share a scripture with you from Mark's writing. I want to take you to chapter twelve, and I want to read verses 13-17, but I want to call your attention to verse fifteen for a message for today:

"And they send unto him certain of the Pharisees and of the Herodians, to catch him in his words. And when they were come, they say unto him, Master, we know that thou art true, and carest for no man: for thou regardest not the person of men, but teachest the way of God in truth: Is it lawful to give tribute to Caesar, or not? Shall we give, or shall we not give? But he, knowing their hypocrisy, said unto them, Why tempt ye me? bring me a penny, that I may see it. And they brought it. And he saith unto them, Whose is this image and superscription? And they said unto him, Caesar's. And Jesus answering said unto them, Render to Caesar the things that are Caesar's, and to God the things that are God's. And they marveled at him." (KJV)

The 15th verse again says, *"Shall we give, or shall we not give? But he, knowing their hypocrisy, said unto them, why tempt ye me? Bring me a penny, that I may see it."* Now with that scripture reading, I want to talk this morning about, "Small Things." Small things, bring me a penny. Christ always paid close attention to little things. He wasn't always favoring the big offerings, the big donations, the big whatever it is you had to give. What He wanted to find in us, was whatever we could give, must come from the heart. And so He says to them when they talked about, 'they should give,' do we honor Caesar or God? And Jesus took the smallest coin He could find and said, *"whose image is on this coin."* They said Caesars. *"Well then I say unto you, render to Caesar what is Caesar's, and render to God what is God's."*

Christ concerns Himself with the small things. Things as small and insignificant as mote. Very few of you listening to me will have had the experience of bringing in Cotton Fields. And when you pick a bale of cotton you take it down to the gin, the cotton gin then divides it, which means separating the cotton from seeds. And you could only sell the cotton, the seed must be taken back for planting. There is a fiber between the seed and the cotton, it's called the mote. It was nothing more than the trash that was gathered between the seed and the cotton.

But you know what, we had to use that! We had to make out bed mattresses from the mote that was left after the cotton was ginned, baled, and sold for other purposes; the seed used for planting there was the mote left – the trash.

And somehow Jesus looks at things like that and says there are people in this world that will never rise to the height of success and grandeur. They will always remain at the lower level of life and they will be considered nothing in comparison to those who feel themselves something. But Jesus looks at the mote and blesses it. He looks at things like the jot and tip. There are those of us who know the King's English and know sometimes it only requires a jot to make a point. You don't have to write the word out, you can just put a jot or a tip. Small things make a significant difference. Jesus looks at things like idol words. Idol words can be translated into gossip. Just talking, saying things that mean nothing, just carrying on idly. But it's important to know that sometimes all a person's got is the garbage they picked up from gossip- it's just idle words. Jesus looks at it and says there are those who only speak what shocks and idle words come from their lips.

But then He looks at a thing like a cup of cold water. You don't need the whole gallon, you don't need a whole well, you just need a cup of cold water. And a cup of water can mean more to the human being than the whole well, cause all you needed was a cup of cold water/ Jesus said we ought to be ready to give a cup of water – small things. Small things represent great principles. Coins are often very valuable depending on what they are made of. If you want a woman to fall in love, give her a diamond. It's a small coin that is the hardest of hard, but it has nothing in it but the light of its development, and however you cast it and move it about it shines with a glow that cannot be matched by any other coin.

And the larger the diamond, the more light it reflects, the more it makes you love or what have you, but the coin is a small item. Jesus declares that when you look at the light of man when you look at people giving and what have you, it is equivalent to giving a coin of great value. Have you ever noticed that a small straw, just a straw can be waved and will show you the direction of the wind? Just hold the straw and you can then determine which way the wind blows. Or something as small as a leaf, a leaf can show you the direction of the oceans flow- put it in the water, and it will declare which direction the water flows. Weather its east, west, north, or south-just a small leaf can determine which way the water flows.

I look at wars that are raging all over the world every now and then. Men and women are now in battle fighting for their rights. But no matter how violent the war is, or how big it rages, somebody in command can take a white flag, raise it up, and stop a war. Small things mean great principles.

Small Things

We are encouraged to bring small things to life in this world. Small things. That just takes a number of us doing little things. I never will forget when I was doing my studies for my Doctoral Dissertation, I looked at the path that black colleges had taken across the years. We had come to a point where we were blessed to be able go to any college or university we could afford to go to. But there was a time when we had no ability to go where we chose to go. We had to go where we could. But the church itself was the hotbed for education, and not only did we worship in spirit and in truth, our parents saved pennies and developed colleges and universities for us to go to.

We are encouraged to bring small things to life in this world. Small things. That just takes a number of us doing little things. I never will forget when I was doing my studies for my Doctoral Dissertation, I looked at the path that black colleges had taken across the years. We had come to a point where we were blessed to be able to go to any college or university we could afford to go to. But there was a time when we had no ability to go where we chose to go. We had to go where we could. But the church itself was the hotbed for education, and not only did we worship in spirit and in truth, our parents saved pennies and developed colleges and universities for us to go to. And by the time I was graduating from college, the black church had already developed more than 80 colleges and universities in America to educate their children. They didn't have much, the offering was pennies and nickels.

And then they would do all of the other things to keep the college going; fixed the building with their own hands, they would raise the food, and plant it in gardens, can it, take it down to the colleges and universities for the students to have something to eat. It didn't cost a lot then. It was just small things being put together that God can bless, and you would be amazed at what God can do with a person fully dedicated.

Small things. Jesus was one day talking to the disciples, and they had a bunch of little kids running around trying to get close to Him and touch Him. The disciples said to them, get back children, He don't have time for that. Jesus looked at His disciples and said, *"suffer the little children to come unto me and forbid them not, for such is the kingdom of heaven. Except you become as a little child you cannot enter the Kingdom of Heaven."* (Mark 10:14) He loved little children.

And then one day He was sitting in the Sanctuary, and people were walking around to pay their tithes and offerings, giving for a blessing. And He looked at the crowd coming with great sums, they had their wealth, their checks, all of the things they needed to make their present. But Jesus looked at a person and said to His disciples, *'come here, I want to show you something.'* What is it Lord? *'That little old woman just came by, and did you see the offering she put in?'* Lord, you can't be serious, she didn't put but three pennies in there! Look at all this money and stuff that we got from other folks. What are you talking about? He said, *'you don't understand, these people who gave large sums gave of their much. Now this woman gave all she had.'* Little things, small things but they are great in principle. She didn't come for no bragging, she didn't want nobody to come by and say thank you to her. She just knew that she had a few pennies to do what she could... And she gave what she had, and Jesus saw it as a major blessing. She didn't just give three pennies, but she gave *all she had.*

I'm gonna close with a few more things that Jesus would look at. He said, Jesus was interested in not only your wealth and stuff, but small things come in all kinds of packages. Jesus says, bring me your heartaches, and let me fix those before they turn into heart attacks- that's my paraphrasing Him. But whatever is bothering you, bring it to Jesus, and He can fix it. He says not only your heartaches, but bring me your little disappointments. We are disappointed every day of our life for one reason or another. We can't handle the disappointments that come our way most of the time, and so all we need is somebody to help us. And Jesus says, bring me your troubles, and I will fix them. Bring me your trials. Your trials can turn into real burdens. Somebody one day wrote a song that says bring your burdens to the Lord, and leave them there. He believes in helping with small things that amount to great things over the long haul. Just a few things. Whatever your trouble is, whatever your trials are, whatever the problem you may face, not only this day, but yesterday, the day before, the day after that. Jesus said, bring me a penny, and I want you to tell me whose image is on it. They said, Caesars. Jesus says, well I'm not telling you don't give Caesar nothing. But I'm telling you to give Caesar what's Caesar's, and what's Gods to God.

God Bless You

Holding On and Growing Stronger

"He shall receive the blessing from the Lord, and righteousness from the God of his salvation." Psalm 24:5

✝ Holding On and Growing Stronger

"For our message today, let me share a scripture from the 24th Psalm, and let me just read that to get us started: The earth is the Lord's, and the fulness thereof; the world, and they that dwell therein. For he hath founded it upon the seas, and established it upon the floods. Who shall ascend into the hill of the Lord? or who shall stand in his holy place? He that hath clean hands, and a pure heart; who hath not lifted up his soul unto vanity, nor sworn deceitfully. He shall receive the blessing from the Lord, and righteousness from the God of his salvation. This is the generation of them that seek him, that seek thy face, O Jacob. Selah. Lift up your heads, O ye gates; and be ye lift up, ye everlasting doors; and the King of glory shall come in. Who is this King of glory? The Lord strong and mighty, the Lord mighty in battle. Lift up your heads, O ye gates; even lift them up, ye everlasting doors; and the King of glory shall come in. Who is this King of glory? The Lord of hosts, he is the King of glory. Selah."

That is to say Amen. Let me share with you a message I'm titling, "Holding on and Growing Stronger" Two of our great messengers of time, David who is responsible for most of the Book of Psalms, and the writings and teachings of Job in a crisis time and how God brought him from one degree to another in a powerful way, and he couldn't help but to testify to the greatness and goodness of God. Job describes life as rising from pessimism to hope and confidence. And all of us have experienced, many times, a very pessimistic life, especially situations that we can't seem to control, or to get a handle on. So we come to a point where we start to feel that everything is lost. That nothing you do is acceptable, and you can't seem to overcome the feeling that even if you try, you fail. And so Job pointed out in his story and gives us a double picture that talks about the righteous holding his way, and man with clean hands growing stronger and stronger.

But in the Psalm, David points out that the Earth is the Lord's, and the fullness thereof; the world, and they that dwell therein. For he hath founded it upon the seas, and established it upon the floods. Who shall ascend into the hill of the Lord? Or who shall stand in his Holy Place? He that hath clean hands, and a pure heart; who hath not lifted up his soul unto vanity, nor sworn deceitfully. He shall receive the blessing from the Lord, and righteousness from the God of his salvation. And so we want to share with you how to just hold on. The righteous gently going forward.

Opposition can many times knock us down. Seems like every time we've got a foot hold we move one step then make a second step, then get knocked back a step. But we have to recognize that opposition will come. See, satan has always performed in the opposition state. He's always taken the position that we are not truly God's, we would rather be ourselves. And that we are out there looking for a leader, and satan says, I'm available. I'll be there for you. God is saying, you can take what they got, but you leave them to Me. And so we find ourselves getting up so often after being knocked down.

But a Christian is not just rushing madly forward. We recognize sometimes that we just have to be still and know that He is God. For we recognize that they that wait on the Lord shall renew their strength. They shall mount us with wings as eagles, run and not be weary, walk and not faint. So the Christian don't just rush about madly trying to get to where they're going. They give God time to work it out. The righteous are not turned aside by obstacles. Everywhere you go, everywhere you step, you have obstacles in your way, stumbling blocks that keep knocking you down, and you keep trying to get up again from day to day. But the Christian recognizes that even at your best, you're going to have obstacles following you, and have you stumbling over them as you go from day to day.

The righteous are not hanging back in fear and weariness. When we know we've got God on our side, we don't just give up and say, "I can't." We stand still and say, God can, and God will make a way. The righteous person pursues a continuous course. They hold on till the end. We must have a purpose in our lives, and not be broken and become failures because we could not do what we thought we could.

See, the righteous person is persistent. They persevere. The righteous person, I think they got their mind on a song that they like to give to people in their troubled times; If you just hold out till tomorrow. If you just keep the faith through the night. If you just hold out till tomorrow, everything will be alright. That's what the righteous will tell you to do on any given occasion. The righteous walk with the right character. Only a man with moral and spiritual character will have the strength to hold on when troubles come. So if you just hold on till tomorrow, if you just keep the faith through the night.

David and Job say in a combination that you have to recognize that this is God's world. The Earth is the Lords. And not just the Earth but the fullness thereof, the world and they that dwell therein. As James Weldon Johnson would say when God got through building this Universe according to His specifications, He said, now let us make man: "From the banks of the river He scooped the clay, by the banks of the river He kneeled Him down, and made man in His own image and likeness, and into him He blew the breath of life. And man became a living soul." The righteous knows you've got to hang on to God's unchanging hand that He gives you the strength to hold continuously when you are tried. And then not only does He give you the ability to hold on, He says you will grow stronger as you hold on. The Christian course is more than a race. You don't have level ground to run on. When you're a Christian you recognize that life itself is an ascend, it goes upward. You will never be able to just cry out—I'm at level ground and I'll be alright.

No, you learn that you've got to walk up the hill, slowly, step by step. You've got to rise each day of your life knowing that mountains are out there to be climbed, and hills are hard. It's not only an ascend, it's growth that you expect from day to day.

I enjoy watching a child grow from that little infant that they were and how humbly they stumble around trying to crawl, falling flat on their face many times. And then one day when the strength of crawling worked out for them, they stood up. You know that's growth. Sometimes you've got to lay in the arms of somebody. Sometimes you've got to crawl on the floor until you're able to stand up, and walk on your feet and then you find yourself stumbling.

Every one of us recognizes that in God we had a beginning, and we have a mountain to climb all the way from Earth to Heaven. And so its growth one day at a time. I look at myself, and I realize I am not what I was, and I know that I'm not now what I've got to be. But it's a climb, it's an ascend, it's moving powerfully onward. Its growth in myself and among others.

There is no monotony in a true Christian's life. I want to say that again. Sometimes we say everything is just so monotonous. I'm just tired of doing the same thing all the time. Life in the Christian world is an ever changing atmosphere. It moves from one degree to another, and it's never downward, it's always upward. And so we have to be sure that we keep on working for the cause. We must learn that we must endure hardships like a good soldier. I don't care how you fight it, sometimes it's hard. I don't care how much love you give, sometimes it's hard. I don't care what you think about tomorrow, you've got to finish today.

He enlarges and enriches us from one day to another. See the Christian grows in strength. Speaking of these two men that I mentioned in the scriptures Job and David in Psalms. Job lost his wealth, but he gained strength. See, he messed around there and got satan on top of him, and satan took all of the stuff that he had. God told him, don't touch his life. And Job went from wealth to poverty, and hung on in bad times.

One day God was standing in front of him. And Job asked Him, why are you doing me like this? Why allow my life to go into turmoil like this? And God asked him, *'Job, where were you when I built the foundation of the Earth. Tell Me, where were you, when the Sons of God shouted for joy. Where were you?'* Job thought, Imma leave Him alone, cause He's been around for a while, and He's got power in His hands, that I need some strength from. So, he lost his wealth, but he gained his strength.

The blows of adversity make the soul tough. See, sometimes we need trouble. Sometimes we need trials and tribulations. Sometimes we need pain and sorrow. Because out of all of those things comes the power to make your soul strong! I will wait on the Lord, no matter what the problem is, no matter where my strength lies, no matter! I'm gonna wait on Him, till my change comes! And so, as you look at your life, you recognize that the blows of adversity will make your soul tough. Bunyan in his Pilgrim's Progress wrote, " That as I walk through the wilderness of this world, I lighted upon a place where was a den, and I lay me down to sleep, and as I slept I dreamt a dream, and in my dream I saw a man clothed with rags. He had a burden on his back, and a book in his hand. And I heard him with a great lamentable cry, say what must I do to be saved? Bunyan went on to point out the Christian when he took on the responsibility of going on this journey that God had sent him on, saying he came to a hill that was called difficulty- and what you have to understand in the Christian journey- God makes the hill difficult to climb.

You've tried to climb high places, high walls or whatever it is, hills you were trying to get over, or mountains, you went out mountain climbing and every time you'd step, look like you stumble, and you tumble down, and you had to dig in again, and start all over again. But you recognize you've got to make it to the top of that mountain, and its hill difficulty is in your way- but, you've got to keep on trusting Him every step of the way. God gives strength to those who have no strength. And He gives man with clean hands a forgiven sin- he has purged his heart.

And so, when you look at this scripture we read; there is an admonishment there by David: "Lift up your heads, O ye gates; and be ye lift up, ye everlasting doors; and the King of glory shall come in." Somebody asked the question, "Who is this King of glory?" The answer comes back from David: "Who is this King of Glory? The Lord strong and mighty, the Lord mighty in battle. Lift up your heads, O ye gates; even lift them up, ye everlasting doors; and the King of glory shall come in." Who did you say this King of glory is? The Lord of hosts, he is the King of glory. Selah. That is to say, Amen. Hanging On and Growing Stronger.

God Bless You

The Harvest is Ripe

"Now let the sickle do its work; the harvest is ripe and waiting. Tread the winepress, for it is full to overflowing with the wickedness of these men." Joel 3:13

† The Harvest is Ripe

Let me share with you a scripture from a book that is little used and read in the Old Testament, I want to come from Joel a small short book but I want to read from Chapter 3, verses 12 through 16:

"Collect the nations; bring them to the valley of Jehoshaphat, for there I will sit to pronounce judgment on them all. Now let the sickle do its work; the harvest is ripe and waiting. Tread the winepress, for it is full to overflowing with the wickedness of these men." Multitudes, multitudes waiting in the valley for the verdict of their doom! For the Day of the Lord is near, in the Valley of Judgment. The sun and moon will be darkened and the stars withdraw their light. The Lord shouts from his Temple in Jerusalem, and the earth and sky begin to shake. But to his people Israel, the Lord will be very gentle. He is their Refuge and Strength." (KJV)

In verse 13 again it says, *"Now let the sickle do its work; the harvest is ripe and waiting. Tread the winepress, for it is full to overflowing with the wickedness of these men."* With that I want to talk about, "The

Harvest is Ripe." Joel is alluding here to a coming judgment in which the results of men's sins would appear and each would reap as he had sown. Every year is fraught with instruction to us reminding us of the bounty that supplies our needs. The fidelity which remains and reminds us of our toil. The certainty of retribution and the reward of our faithfulness. The harvest is ripe.

We generally expect to bear fruit from the seeds we plant and we decide what will be planted. What seeds we expect to germinate, sprout at the root and come up from the root and grow the fruit that we desire. And every year God reminds us through His seasons that He is in charge of harvest time. Whatever we plant, we shall sow and whatever we sow, we will harvest. You cannot expect to harvest crops you did not plant. You cannot expect to gather fruit from one tree expecting the fruit of another tree. The harvest reveals the results of man's labor. The Bible teaches us that whatsoever a man soweth that shall he also reap. He which soweth sparingly shall reap sparingly. He which soweth bountifully shall reap also bountifully.

We see this in our social life. When it comes to reaping the harvest sown by us and others. A nation that allows its children to grow up in poverty to have nothing to look forward to but a little of nothing from day to day. A nation that allows decency to be impossible. Where nobody believes in right and righteousness. Don't give time for people to develop a loving relationship within their community. A nation that provides little or no knowledge and virtue in learning, Give the worst to the least. Give just enough to say, I gave.

I will never forget, I know I got people listening to me that know a little something about it but, a whole lotta people don't know that the school we attended when I was growing up; I remember the Science Lab real well. We had one frog and one snake in the Science Lab. And right down the road in walking distance almost five miles from my school, the white schools had a lab with all of the various learning tools and techniques in it. Just five miles away. And what we had to learn in science, had to be learned from a little of nothing. And then we are expected to know as much, and learn as much as anybody else in a separate and unequal school. You can't expect to allow your children to grow up in huddles of poverty, and where they are not able to live in a decent environment and they are not able to gain the knowledge and virtue needed to become decent citizens. What can you expect when you look at the crime on the streets? What can you expect when you run out of jail cells? You got to put more money into building jails because you refuse to put money into educating the young. What can you expect more than misery?

Look at not only our social life but our intellectual life. You will reap what you sow. I can recall that in the absence of good schools, and good laboratories, and good things, books and things used in learning that we had parents that taught us the basics of education. We may not have been able to do Algebra, Geometry and all the other things that have technical parts to it, but we knew how to count: one, two, three. We knew how to read: A, B, C. And if you keep on reading them long enough you could put words together that make sense to you. And some of us turned out alright. You can't gain a good education from just simply copying somebody else. You can't just look over at the next person's paper and write what they've written. You might end up copying their name! You can't dodge and duck study.

Paul said once study to show thyself approved. A workman that needed not be ashamed, rightly dividing the word of truth. It comes hard, sometimes it's rough, but you've got to apply yourself and learn all you can to get where you're trying to go. Wisdom is the principal thing. Therefore get wisdom, but in all thy getting, get an understanding. The nation who looks at the occupations provided don't realize that you only reap what you sow. We tend to somehow believe that we all can be rich or famous and we look at those who made it and decide, I want to be that kind of person too. But whatever you choose to become as a result of the choice you make and the stick-to-itiveness that you applied. In other words, make your choice of what seed you're gonna plant, what fruits you gonna grow, and be persistent at it every day of your life.

Look at our spiritual life. If we can apply ourselves to our social life, and our work life- all of the things we do in life, we can also apply ourselves to a spiritual life. How will we do that? Christ has already provided the method by which we can have, and live a spiritual existence and He didn't just leave it to our chance.

If you want a spiritual life, He will give us the seed of truth, so that we can grow up knowing the difference in right and wrong. He provides the seed of truth. And I'll tell you something else, He will do; He will prepare the soil of our hearts. I wondered many times as I dug through the scriptures and tried to find the answers that were pressing, how would Christ expect us to change the heart of man? He told us to go and teach all nations, baptizing them in the name of the Father, Son, and Holy Ghost. He said teach them to observe all things, whatsoever I have commanded you. And lo, I am with you always, even till the end of the world.

And so, if I go, and I meet hostile and violent men and women, how will I be able to get inside of their hearts? Jesus said, '*if you go, I will put the seed in you to plant in their heart, and I will prepare their heart to receive your planting.*' And then He said, not only will I put the seed of truth in you to sow, and I will prepare the soil of their heart, I will water what you have sown. Everything needs water. Jesus says, 'I'll put the seed in you, I'll touch their heart and get them ready, and then I will water it with My grace.'

If Christ is going to do all of that for us, what are we going to do for Him? For just as sure as you sow your seeds, the day of retribution will surely come. There is an old proverb that says that he that seeketh mischief it shall come upon him. I thought about Haman in the Bible, Haman was so hateful to the Jews that he wanted to kill all of them. And he wanted to start with their leader. And he went out and built a gallows- something you hang people on and he was going to summarily kill everybody in the Jewish community. And he got the word out, and word to around that he was that treacherous and he had started killing people at will. One day the queen stopped by to see him. And the queen whispered in his ear, Haman, I'm a Jew too. And when the word got out that he was killing all Jews, the queen had been brought to the kingdom and she's a Jew. Haman was hanged on his own gallows. When you plot somebody else's destruction, you are plotting your own. His vaulting ambition, over-lapped himself. And what you sow, you gone reap.

And there was another group of people, the men of Babel sought to defy God. I had to look that up again cause I was surprised with what was happening with the Nation of people. God had sent the men of Babel to bring His word to all nations and to place themselves across the universe- and they didn't want to do that. And then I remembered as I read that this was Noah's son. God had already had Noah to build an Ark-keep the people alive, and his family was the selected group to be on that water until the water went down, and God called upon them to spread His name and His word on all the land. And they decided they didn't want to split up. They didn't want to leave home. And they had what is considered engineering capabilities, they were smart people, and instead of them taking the word of God to every part of the Earth, they decided they would just build a ladder from Earth to Heaven, and they would just climb on up there.

The men of Babel sought to defy God and brought about their own scattering. Here's what happened: They were so smart that as they built the ladder to heaven, they built it higher and higher because they had a certain brick that they had to use to get it there. And the further they raised that stairway to Heaven the further they got away from the language that everybody could speak. By the time they got themselves a little bit too high, they couldn't even understand what the men at the top were sending down as a question to answer what supplies they needed down on the ground. The language changed. You've been in situations like that. When you've talked as long as you could stand it, and then you realized you didn't even know the language of the person standing by you. But when they tried to defy God, and not do what He told them to do – go into all the world and teach all nations. They decided no, we don't want to split up. We're gonna stay together. So they just kept building upward, and the language changed, and they couldn't even understand what they were saying to each other.

There was another group, and I'm going to leave you alone. The Pharisees one day. See you had two sets of people called the Pharisees and Sadducees. The Sadducees were known as the educated crowd. The people who stayed socially connected. The Pharisees were the religious order. Those who served the Lord and kept the faith, and kept working for His Kingdom. One day Jesus came and Jesus was including everybody into His world and His word. But the Pharisees He was taking over from them, and they needed Him out of the way. So they crucified the Son of God. They made His cross the pivot of the world's history. When you try to kill God, you're creating a world that you don't even understand yourself, and you can't handle God.

So when you crucify Jesus, you have touched the Son of God, and God will not allow His Son to be killed. Put ye in the sickle, the harvest is ripe. In other words, I'm calling all Kingdoms together in the valley of

Jehoshaphat. And I will deal with their differences and their inability to get along with one another.

And so what you do is simply take the sickle, it's time to gather the harvest. I want all people to be brought together, and I will decide what happens to them in the end. Church the harvest is ripe. We've sown the seed, we've tilled the ground. We've cultivated it as far as we can do it, and God has granted the watering of our sowing, and now He tells us, the harvest is ripe. I just want to advise you, if you planted apples, don't look for oranges. If you planted collards, don't look for turnips. If you planted sin, don't look for grace. If you planted the wrong seed for the crop you wanted to gather, you have to know in your own heart and mind, be not deceived, God is not marked. Whatsoever a man soweth, that shall he also reap.

God Bless You

The Anakims

"Now therefore give me this mountain, whereof the LORD spake in that day; for thou heardest in that day how the Anakims were there, and that the cities were great and fenced: if so be the LORD will be with me, then I shall be able to drive them out, as the LORD said."
Joshua 14:12

The Anakims

Let me share with you a scripture from the book of Joshua. I'm taking you to the fourteenth chapter and I'm going to use the twelfth verse as a basis for the message. But I want to read a few verses of that fourteenth chapter surrounding that particular verse, starting with verse seven:

"Forty years old was I when Moses the servant of the LORD sent me from Kadeshbarnea to espy out the land; and I brought him word again as it was in mine heart. Nevertheless my brethren that went up with me made the heart of the people melt: but I wholly followed the LORD my God. And Moses sware on that day, saying, Surely the land whereon thy feet have trodden shall be thine inheritance, and thy children's for ever, because thou hast wholly followed the LORD my God. And now, behold, the LORD hath kept me alive, as he said, these forty and five years, even since the LORD spake this word unto Moses, while the children of Israel wandered in the wilderness: and now, lo, I am this day fourscore and five years old.

The Anakims

As yet I am as strong this day as I was in the day that Moses sent me: as my strength was then, even so is my strength now, for war, both to go out, and to come in. Now therefore give me this mountain, whereof the LORD *spake in that day; for thou heardest in that day how the Anakims were there, and that the cities were great and fenced: if so be the* LORD *will be with me, then I shall be able to drive them out, as the* LORD *said."* (KJV)

Let me talk a few minutes about the Anakims in our life. You have heard that the Anakims were there. The story of Joshua's rendering of the mountain that was to be given to an old friend of his. They had been assigned by Moses, to go over, and spy the land and come back, and bring a report as to whether that land could be taken by Israel as God had promised.

Caleb and Joshua were assigned to make that journey along with ten other men. When they went to check out the land that Moses was interested in knowing the condition of the battle that would need to be fought to acquire that land. When they came back with their report ten of those twelve men gave a negative report. They said to Moses, 'Moses we think you ought to leave that land alone because the Anakims are there.' And these were men who were known to be the offspring of Annach; who had been given a portion of land as their inheritance, and Annach had three sons that were structured like giants. They were huge in body and they called them, "stiff necked men." That they could fight a battle like none other. And they had fortified the city, so that no people or no person could come into that

The Anakims

area without being known, being spotted, and being taken care of, and gotten rid of. And so they had fortified their land, and learned to fight the battles that the others not only respected but feared.

But when Joshua had been placed instead of Moses; he had inherited the charge to keep that Moses left. One day when the sons of God came to reap their harvest, get their inheritance Joshua was passing out land, areas and cities to people who came from the various tribes, and there in the midst of that crowd was his old friend Caleb. Caleb walked up to him and said, Joshua, you remember me. You remember the promise that Moses made to me. He promised me the land where my feet had trod. He would give me my own inheritance from that mountain range up there. And I don't want you to look at my age. I feel just as strong today, as I did forty-five years ago when you heard Moses say to me that I could have the mountain. And I want you to know that I trusted God then, and I trust Him now. I want you to give me that mountain. And I shall go, and my people will inherit that land. He put in a little point that all Christians ought to recognize; if God be with me, I can take it. Don't you worry about my age or my condition! I'm counting on God delivering that land to me. And I couldn't help but take the word Anakim, and the men that made up that environment; who fought battles and won them, and then fortified their territory so nobody else could come in, and they stood the test well. Over the time that they had it before Caleb declared, give me this mountain.

You can't help but realize that you have to compare that fighting army that battles to those great warriors who stood the test of time, and who could take their land and fortify it, so people would be afraid to go near them. And they said they are strong and mighty. They are stiff necked men. Caleb said, don't worry about their stiff-neckness and about my age. Give me this mountain. And if God is for me, I'll take it.

As we live in this world all of us will have Anakims in our inheritance. Some of our highest blessings are fenced about with the greatest difficulties. Sometimes you have to realize that what God's got for you, you've got to fight for it. What God's got to give you is yours for the asking, but you've got to go out and apply yourself into the world that God has provided, and God will provide. And so sometimes our highest blessing is all fenced in by the greatest difficulties.

No earthly inheritance is without peculiar disadvantages. *No earthly inheritance is without peculiar disadvantages.* What you get, you've got to work for it. What you hold on to, you've got to fight for it. You've got to realize that there is a disadvantage to every advantage that comes your way. And so the Anakims in our life are similar to the Anakims in Caleb's life -- they are stiff necked and giant like. And we've got to know that we've got to fight to overcome them. Some of the Anakims which resist us are our efforts to fulfill our mission. And the efforts that we have in fulfilling our mission sometimes is thwarted by the evils of our own heart. Sometimes we are our worst enemy. Sometimes we are held back not because somebody else did it, but because we did it. Our earthly inheritance has disadvantages and they are peculiar to us, but to the Anakims that resist us in our effort to fulfill our mission, many times is nothing more than the evil in our own heart.

We've got to overcome ourselves first. We've got to become what God has desired for us in our lifetime through our struggles and our dedication to His will and His word. And so, we too, must resist the Anakims in our life. You may have in your heart the indolence and the fear that often beset us. In other words, you ought not just want to live for pleasure, having a good time in a good place. You ought to realize that in order for you to achieve, to accomplish what God desires for you to have, you've got to get up on your feet and stand up like a man or a woman and be what God requires of you. For we cannot just live in the fear that if I try somebody else is gonna take what I got and I'm gonna be overcome and over run by people who are my enemy.

Now Caleb didn't say, 'I might get the mountain.' Caleb said give me this mountain, and if the Lord be with me, I'll take it. Now he knew that he had to fight off fear, he had to fight off earthliness. He had to fight off the temptations of the world. He had to go out and fight for what God is granting him.

Sometimes the Anakims can take control of our life by bad examples. See Caleb had to worry about the giant men. The men who knew how to fight in battle and who could win wars of all types. But sometimes our greatest battle is a bad example that somebody set for us. You can't allow yourself to be overrun by somebody that doesn't care about your existence in the first place.

Sometimes we are overrun through the Anakim world through the customs we are accustomed to. Many of us have some old bad habits. We learned them the easy and hard way. We just grew up in the custom of doing things this or that way and never seeking to change the way we do things. Customs can destroy you, for you want to be like what you've seen in others, But no, you've got to step away like Caleb And say that you were with me Joshua when the 10 men came back with negative reports and said we shouldn't even try it, we can't do it; the city is fortified, the men are giants, and they are stiff necked. But I want you to know that I'm willing to take on this charge and you give me the mountain.

But it's best for us as it was to have such an inheritance. God is there for us to inherit what He's got for us. Let me tell you a few things about the difficulties of acquiring and accepting your inheritance. One of the difficulties of trying to achieve what Gods got for you is that it tries your faith. Faith in God is important. Faith in God under adverse circumstances is always something you need to understand. You've got to keep fine- tuned .If you lose your faith, you've lost your ability to accomplish the mountain. Faith is the substance of things hoped for, it's the evidence of things not seen. But if you allow the difficulty to take your faith, you've lost your battle before you even start. There's the difficulty of losing your courage. Trembling, scared to death you can't do it, I won't try. No, you better fine tune your faith, Pray to God to help you. Pick-up yourself, your courage, and fight that battle that He's placed before you. Because if you keep your faith strong and your courage right, God will give you the scope of energy that you need for the destination.

Make the ultimate peace the more blessed. If you fight the battle in faith, with the courage of Jesus Christ, then you will find energy and devotion for your journey, and it will give you ultimate peace as you're blessed with your mountain. Difficulties in our life can rob us of our willingness to do good, and do right, and do well. Sometimes, the difficulties of life can make you leave the work you've got going in the church. If you lose your faith, and your courage, your church work will suffer. And Jesus Christ has called upon us to, "go into all the world, and teach all nations, baptize them in the name of the Father, the Son, and the Holy Ghost. Teach them to observe all things, whatsoever I have commanded you and Lo, I am with you always, even unto the end of the world."

We have means of overcoming the Anakims. Caleb knew that, and look at how he put it. 'If God be with me, I shall take the mountain. God is with us,' and this is what the ground of confidence that Caleb had. If I got God on my side, I got everything I need. Nobody can stop me, nobody can prevent me from overcoming the circumstances of my life, if God be with me.

God doesn't just approve of the right. He aids it. Now you know that all of these eighty five years that Caleb had lived with God he did the bidding of God, he had enough experience to know that there was nothing in this world that God couldn't do. And all he had to do was keep his hands in the hands of the Man who can still the waters. He certainly could give him success on that mountain. So God doesn't just approve of the right, He aids it. God doesn't merely send assistance for the battle of life, He's present. You know we, we sometimes say in a kind way, that if God be with me, I'll go... But you ought to know God is with you, not if. You ought to know God is with you, and with God being with you, He will not just send you into the battle of life, He's present with you. God will go with us in life's battle, and stand and give us the strength to fight battles in His name... I shall be able, Caleb says, to drive them out with God's help. He didn't say, I'm bad. He didn't say I got enough strength to go in there and take that mountain. He said, Moses promised it to me, and for the past forty five years I have been counting on it. I was forty years old when I got that promise. I'm eighty five now. And you know something, I don't feel any weaker now than I did forty five years ago. And the God who promised me through Moses that mountain down yonder when I was much younger, is the same God who can give it to me now. And so I shall be able to drive the Anakims out not with my own hands, but with God's help.

Ours is the effort, God is the strength. If you go, and ask God to go with you, there is no hill that you can't climb, no valley you can't cross. There is no river wide enough or deep enough to hinder God from getting you where you're going. You provide the effort, God provides the strength. Get up every morning, go about your business, and do what is right. God will go with you. And when you're falling almost to the ground, the strength of God will pick you up and prop you on every leaning side.

Victory will not be given unless we fight. If you go to the mountain, you go to take it, you know you are going to fight in the first place. All you're asking God to do is, Lord give me the strength, and the know-how, and let me fight this battle. And Lord you prop me when I'm falling. And just the same as Caleb could declare to Joshua on that day, give me this mountain. If God goes with me, I can take it.

Church, wherever you are, wherever your mountain is. No matter how high you've got to climb, how many times you expect to fall, and slide back up to the top of the mountain, go Take God with you. You provide the fight, He will provide the strength.

God Bless You, God Keep You

Our Everlasting Father

"For unto us a child is born, unto us a son is given: and the government shall be upon his shoulder: and his name shall be called Wonderful, Counselor, The mighty God, The everlasting Father, The Prince of Peace." Isaiah 9:6

☦ Our Everlasting Father

Since we're in the midst of a coming celebration of Father's Day, we are buying all of the gifts and cards to honor that day and that moment. I thought it would be a good thing to first introduce the father of us all. I want to take you to the book of Isaiah 9th chapter and 6th verse, and let me just read it:

"For unto us a child is born, unto us a son is given: and the government shall be upon his shoulder: and his name shall be called Wonderful, Counselor, The mighty God, The everlasting Father, The Prince of Peace. Of the increase of his government and peace there shall be no end." (KJV)

So let me just take this time and talk about Our Everlasting Father. We can all relate to Him. He's not color blind. He doesn't pick out individuals that He's nearest to or who's dearest to Him, but it's something we ought to recognize as we celebrate Fatherhood.

When the Messiah is called Father, we must understand that the word means protector. God is our father, He's our maker, our keeper, He is our protector, and He protects all the way down to the inner sanctum of our souls and so there is no separation from this father. When the body decays, somebody said, I have another building, a house not made with hands, eternal in the heavens.

This scripture introduces us to the revealer of God to man. God designed to reveal Himself at last to His creatures through a man's earthly life. Think about it; the God who said, "Let there be light" and there was light. And then said to the Earth, "bring forth", and it brought forth. And then wrapped it up by saying, "Let us make man", and made us in His image, and likeness, and then blew the breath of life into us. On this occasion, Isaiah points out, now man has not only violated his existence with God, but had done it in such a way- the violation, that he had no way back to God. God decided to send a part of Himself to Earth and teach man how to live, how to exist, and how to co-exist, and then have a place in eternity. So if you remember those of you who are Bible students, if you remember when God shared Job with satan, He said to him, "now you can take what you want from him, but don't touch his life, that's mine."

And so God is showing us the way back to Him now, is a part of Him coming to prepare a way of salvation for us so that our souls would be salvaged from all of the dangers that surround us from day to day. The revealer of God to man. God designed to reveal Himself as a man. And so God can only reveal Himself to man or to woman to the extent that he or she seeks to know Him. In other words, God won't just force Himself on you. He's not going to just force you to be His. He will give you the privilege of accepting Him as your Lord and Savior, and He gives you all the reasons why you need to do it. See, to know Jesus is to know God. Often you hear people saying I don't know this God, I don't know how to find Him. I don't know how to get in touch with Him. Jesus came to be God's representative and to show us how we can get to God through Him.

Everywhere and in everything we feel that He is God. He was an outcast baby for whom there was no room in the Inn, yet angels heralded His coming. You remember the story of how when Jesus was born in that stable in Bethlehem, laid in a manger, in a trough that cows were fed from. He was a nobody, and then angels showed up, and sang, Glory, Glory to God in the highest.

To know Jesus is to know God. He was a simple child of 12 years old, yet the temple doctors were astonished at His understanding, and His answers. One day he got mixed up, stayed too long at the temple talking with learned folk, his mother and father looking for Him, at the age of 12, they ran all over town trying to find Jesus. And when they finally found Him, Mary said to Him, "you had me worried. You know that you were not supposed to get lost from us." And Jesus said, "I was about my Father's business. "At the age of twelve God is getting Him ready to show man how to exist in this world.

He submitted Himself to John the Baptist at the River Jordan, and the Holy Ghost descended upon Him. They say the Holy Ghost descended like a dove, and the angels sang again. Jesus, God said to the crowd around, "This is my beloved Son in whom I am well pleased." This Jesus that God is introducing to us in the form of a man wept tears of human friendship, at the grave of a friend, Lazarus. Lazarus got sick unto death, and his two sisters sent for Jesus, who was not in town. And when they gave Him the word, Jesus stayed where He was for a while, and He said to them, "All sickness is not unto death." And then He finally came across the mountain and Lazarus was now in the grave. And Jesus said to the crowd who was following Him at that moment to see what He would do, and what He could do. He said, "Show me where you laid him. And they took Him to the grave. When He got to the grave Jesus simply looked up to Heaven and said, "Father, not for my sake, but for the sake of those standing around, I want you to raise Lazarus." And look at what He did. He didn't even look or wait to get a call back from Heaven; when He said to the Father, 'Father not for my sake but the sake of those standing around I want you to raise Lazarus, and then He simply looked at the grave and said Lazarus, come forth.' God is in the form of a man showing us His powers all the way from the Kingdom. And so Lazarus got up, and came out of that grave, and friendship was restored to the house.

This Jesus died in agony and shame on Calvary as only a man could. But He had promised if you kill me, I'll rise again. And on the third day Jesus rose from the dead, and came declaring all Power in Heaven and on earth is in my hand.

This Jesus that has been introduced to us by Isaiah. Isaiah further said the coming one is a child, but the government shall be on His shoulder. He is a child, and yet He is wonderful. He's a Counselor, A Mighty God, He's A Prince of Peace. He is a Son, and yet it can be said that He is the Everlasting Father. The Son is the Father.

One day He had to say to one of His disciples that was claiming we don't know the Father. Jesus said, "He that has seen me has seen the Father." He did not come as a cherub, or an angel, but as a man. He came as the seed of Abraham. Not as a King. He recognized that kings were sometimes barbarians. And kings were full of blood guiltiness, Kings were full of tyranny and debauchery, and cruelty.

But He came as a Father. One who accepts a weeping prodigal. You remember the man whose son left home. He went and said to his father, " I want you to give me my portion of what we have worked for on this land, and I want you to know I'm going to enjoy myself, I'm going to live my life and I want you to give me what I would receive upon your death- I need it now." And he gave it to him. And the Bible tells us that that son took that wealth and spent it in riotous living. In other words he had a ball, a good time! And when he finished having a ball, he had nothing left. He had to eat from the hogs trough cause he was out of money to buy food. All of the friends he had when he was rich were now gone. They had to find them another fool to work on. And so he was there with nothing. But all of the time that this young man was having a ball with his wealth, his father never gave up hope that he would return home.

Look at this father that God has prepared for this message: Every day he would go to the door and look down the road. He didn't have any postage coming in, no mail to be dropped off. Didn't hear a word from his son, didn't have a phone to get a call-nothing was available to him; he just had in his heart that soon he would return. But the key to it is not so much that the son will return, but that the father's door will be open when he does. And then one day he looked down the road and the son was seen at a distance, raggedy, tattered, torn from the struggle and it was no problem for the father to recognize him afar off. And while the boy was still trying to get there, the father is declaring a point. He said to some of his servants, I want you to go yonder, and prepare a picnic for my son. He was lost, now he's found, he was blind, but now he sees. Go get me the fatted calf and make a meal, cause I want my son to come back and be returned to the house.

Now, when the boy got closer, the daddy looked at him and said, "I don't like the looks of what I see." He said to his servants, "go and bring me a robe to put on him. I want you to get some shoes and put them on his feet. I want something better than what I'm finding coming home. I want you to celebrate my child who was lost and is now found!"

When God becomes your Father and you become a prodigal child, God is always there to welcome you on your way back. He doesn't come out saying, you remember when, you remember what you did. He doesn't come out saying these kinds of things. He comes out saying welcome My child. He holds you in Him arms.

And this everlasting Father that we have accepted goes so far as to wipe away our tears from our eyes. He calls for music and dancing to celebrate the return of a child. And put on the best robe in the house. Our everlasting Father is what God has prepared through His Son Jesus, to represent Him in our lives. In this world no matter what the circumstances, God has prepared a way out for us.

And when it's all over we shall go and be with Him. Isaiah says: *"For unto us a child is born, unto us a son is given: and the government shall be upon his shoulder: and his name shall be called Wonderful, Counselor, mighty God, everlasting Father, Prince of Peace."* (KJV)

Church, it's good to have a permanent replacement. Our earthly fathers can exist only a while, sometimes too short of a time. But even if they live to be a ripe old age, they still cannot live long enough to do what God is able to do for us. And so He has already prepared a place for us so that in His house there is room. And His son is Father of the Universe.

God Bless You

A Man of Sorrow, Acquainted With Grief

"Is it nothing to you, all ye that pass by? behold, and see if there be any sorrow like unto my sorrow, which is done unto me, wherewith the Lord *hath afflicted me in the day of his fierce anger. "*
Lamentations 1:12

† A Man of Sorrow, Acquainted With Grief

Without delay let me take you directly to the message I want to share with you a scripture from Lamentations, first chapter and I want to read the twelfth verse in your hearing:

Is it nothing to you, all ye that pass by? behold, and see if there be any sorrow like unto my sorrow, which is done unto me, wherewith the Lord *hath afflicted me in the day of his fierce anger.* (KJV)

I want to talk for a few minutes from the subject, "A Man of Sorrow, and Acquainted with Grief." We started last Sunday celebrating Father's Day, and I want to touch it again as we give credit to whom credit is due; and to acknowledge the fathers of this world who have given much to the cause of their families and others that they could touch. We tend to give a whole lot more praise and credit to mothers on mother's day, but you ought to know that to be a father one has to be well aware of his place in the heart, and in society. And some of the men of this world do a really good job of dealing with the lives of their children and families, and working it out to their family's best advantage. And while they may not get recognized for it many times, it does exist.

"Is it nothing to you, all ye that pass by? Behold, and see if there be any sorrow like unto my sorrow, which is done unto me." Let me give you the background of this scripture. These words take us back 600 years before Christ came. Jerusalem had fallen. It had been taken by the hand of the Chaldeans, and the city lay in ruins. Jerusalem was much like many of the cities we love in America. It was a city among cities. It was a princess among provinces, it was a nation among nations. Her way had been destroyed, her gates. In other words, if you want to replace that word, her airport terminals are desolate. Her ministers and priests were shaking their heads and sighing because they couldn't do anything about it. The city had been plunged to the lowest depth of despair.

But she raised her head one day and started to appeal to the travelers coming and going from place to place. Some merely to see the devastation of Jerusalem, others to pray for her revival. They appealed not just to the travelers of their care and their help, they appealed to nations around the world. They wanted anybody who had a good feeling about their destiny that they would give them some help to restore the city in the nation.

And when they decided that they had appealed for all the help that humankind could give, they called on God. God answered in a strange way; He sent a part of Himself as a Son. He sent Jesus to take care of human problems. And in the process of sending Him He put His own Son through the trials and tribulations that a man will go through in his life, in order to be a father of families, God showed us first of all that

He was a father of all, and that He sent His Son to ultimately become the Father of Nations. Jesus lived and suffered in the process of His living. Jesus knows pain. Jesus knows hunger. There when He came up out of the Jordan River, John had baptized Him He went into the wilderness to pray, and He prayed 40 days and 40 nights getting in touch with His Father to be sure that the start was right and when He had stayed there 40 days and 40 nights, it dawned on Him that He hadn't even had any food.

And satan was sitting there watching Him. Satan said, 'you know I've had my eyes on you for quite a while, and they tell me that you are the son of God. And I know that you've been out here praying and weeping for all of these days and nights, and I have noticed you haven't eaten anything- and I know you are hungry. Now if you be the Christ, the Son of God, you can show your power right now, and I want you to make these stones turn into bread.' Jesus looked at Him square in the eyes and said, "Man shall not live by bread alone, but by every word that precedes out of the mouth of God." Jesus knows hunger.

Jesus knows thirst. On occasions He would stop by wells and ask for a drink of water. People would sometimes give Him one, other times they would not. They would tell Him that I'm not giving you anything because I'm not a part of your race, I'm not a part of your family. And so you have to get your own water. And Jesus' reply on one occasion was, "you don't know who I am. You need water that I give. I give you living water and you will never thirst again." Jesus knew and knows what it is to wear a crown of thorns and be scourged as an inhuman person.

Jesus was taken to Calvary to be killed there because the world thought they could manage God better, if they could just get rid of Him in public view, and so they hung Him on a cross but before they hung him there, they pressed a crown of thorns on His head, made Him carry the cross up the hill of Golgotha, place called the skull, Calvary. And they scourged Him. They whipped Him, they did all kinds of evil against Him. Women were crying and following Him up that hill of Calvary, and they were begging for help, somebody help the man, don't do that to Him." Jesus stopped in the midst of the scourging, in the midst of the load to Calvary and said, "Daughters of Jerusalem, weep not for me, but weep for yourselves and for your children. For if they do this to a green tree, what will they do to a dry?" He knows scourging.

Jesus knows what it feels like to have nails driven in your hands, spikes in your feet, and then stood up on a cross to bleed and die. But instead of Him just simply giving up, He looked toward heaven while He was up there on that cross, and said, *"Father, forgive them for they know not what they do."*

Jesus knows what a spear feels like going in His side. Somebody decided, No, He's not dead yet, we got to be sure He's dead. And they stuck a spear in His side to let Him bleed out. But He was already gone. Jesus took only three hours to finish that process on Calvary, and then said in very public view, "Father into Thy hands I commend my Spirit."

Jesus knows loneliness. If we dwell upon the details of His physical suffering, it is to divert the thoughts of man from the main source of His character and His suffering. Jesus was rejected in Galilee. People didn't want Him there; from the day of His birth they didn't want Him in the kingdom. Jesus knows loneliness. He was despised in Jerusalem. His friends couldn't understand why He would allow that kind of person, the kind of people to do Him the way they were doing Him. But He went on with His mission, and they couldn't understand why He would do it, and why He would allow it.

God sometimes gives us enough time to wonder out loud, has He left us. While Jesus was hanging on that cross He said, *"My God, My God, why hast Thou forsaken me?"* It just seems like even God had walked away from Him. But He knew He had not.

It would make you wonder if God had allowed Him to stay any longer, He probably would have died feeling that He was left alone to die by Himself. Jesus knows sorrow, but to dwell upon these details of His physical suffering is to divert the thoughts of man from the main source of His character and His suffering. Jesus cried out, "Is it nothing to you, all you that pass by. If there is any sorrow like my sorrow which has been brought on me, which the Lord has inflicted and instilled in the day of His fierce anger.

Jesus knows sorrow. Because He was the man of sorrow, I can now promise you that He is now the King of Glory. See if Jesus hadn't gone through all that to show us how to take the world's trials and tribulations and stay close to the Father in heaven we would not have had the privilege of celebrating fatherhood.

Jesus wept that He might one day wipe away all tears from the eyes of millions. Shortest verse in the Bible says, "Jesus wept." You know it comes from that story that I mentioned just a few weeks ago of Lazarus being in the grave, and Mary and Martha sending for Jesus to come see about him when he was sick, and Jesus didn't come. And they had to bury him in the absence of Jesus, and Jesus came later and said to them, "Show me where you laid him." And they showed Him, and Jesus wept, and then prayed and said, "Father not for My sake, but for the sake of those standing around, raise Lazarus." And then He said to Lazarus, "Come forth."

Jesus wept that He could wipe away all tears from our eyes. He worried that multitudes might rejoice. He's been through it. All of us who suffer in this world, and who believe in Jesus Christ as Lord and Savior know that our suffering is temporary. Our problems will go away, cause He will see to it on the day of reckoning. And so He sorrowed that multitudes might rejoice.

Finally, He shed His blood so that many a bleeding heart might be healed. When you look at the troubles and trials that we go through in this world, the amount of suffering we endure trying to do what is right. We suffer greatly, I don't know why the suffering must be so great, but Jesus shed His blood so that those of us who have bleeding hearts might be healed. A man of sorrow, acquainted with grief.

Men of God, you will suffer in this world, you will have your trials, you will have your temptations, you will have your woes. But Jesus is showing us that even that's bearable. Whatever it is somebody put on you, oh you can stand up again, and say I'm in the presence of my Lord, and He will provide, and He will take care of me.

Jesus knows pain. Jesus knows loneliness. Jesus knows sorrow, and as the speaker in the scripture stated, He wondered out loud, it is nobody else's sorrow that I have, and we all feel we have to do this, carry this load alone. But it's not true, because God provided us away out of all the aches and pains and suffering and sorrow that we must endure.

May God Bless you and Keep you!

God's Design of Men

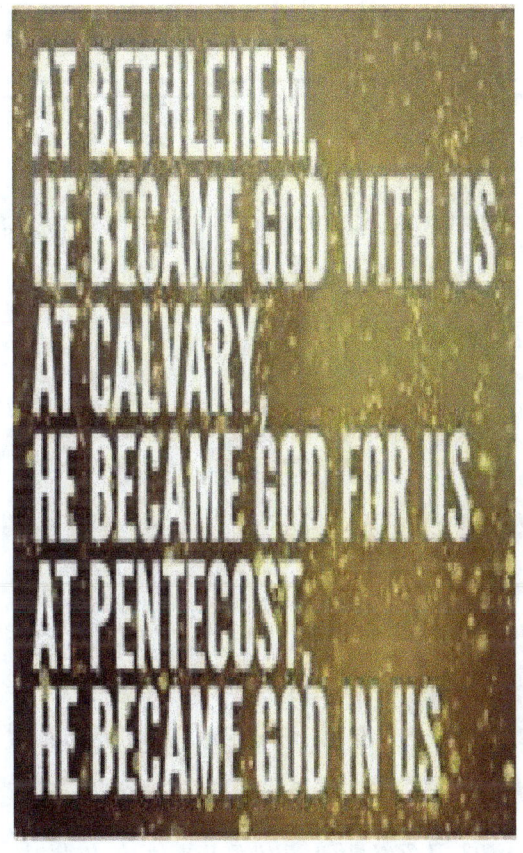

I will praise thee; for I am fearfully and wonderfully made: marvelous are thy works; and that my soul knoweth right well."
Psalm 139:14

✝ God's Design of Men

For our message today, let me take you to Psalm. Psalm number 139, and I want to read a great portion of that psalm in your hearing, beginning with verse one:

"O lord, thou hast searched me, and known me. Thou knowest my downsitting and mine uprising, thou understandest my thought afar off. Thou compassest my path and my lying down, and art acquainted with all my ways. For there is not a word in my tongue, but, lo, O Lord, thou knowest it altogether. Thou hast beset me behind and before, and laid thine hand upon me. Such knowledge is too wonderful for me; it is high, I cannot attain unto it. Whither shall I go from thy spirit? or whither shall I flee from thy presence? If I ascend up into heaven, thou art there: if I make my bed in hell, behold, thou art there. If I take the wings of the morning, and dwell in the uttermost parts of the sea; Even there shall thy hand lead me, and thy right hand shall hold me. If I say, Surely the darkness shall cover me; even the night shall be light about me. Yea, the darkness hideth not from thee;

but the night shineth as the day: the darkness and the light are both alike to thee. For thou hast possessed my reins: thou hast covered me in my mother's womb. I will praise thee; for I am fearfully and wonderfully made: marvellous are thy works; and that my soul knoweth right well." (KJV)

I want to use that 14th verse as a basis of the message, "I will praise thee; for I am fearfully and wonderfully made: marvellous are thy works; and that my soul knoweth right well." I want to talk about, "God's design of men." The psalmist says again, *"I will praise thee; for I am fearfully and wonderfully made: marvellous are thy works; and that my soul knoweth right well."* Look at God's design of men. Only you can be you. Think about it. God developed a plan, the architectural plan for you in existence, and gave us our own fingerprints. Nobody can match your fingerprint. And then He gave us our own DNA. It makes us uniquely different from everything and everybody God created. So there is no duplication. You can't say, make me a copy of that, and it comes out with the same message. God made us individuals, and made us uniquely different from each other.

You ever wondered how come two women can bake the same cake, and they come out tasting different; using the same recipe. It's something about what one puts in hers, against what the other puts in hers that makes it uniquely different and the taste comes out differently. Same cake, made in the same pan, mixed with batter out of the same type but you can tell the difference in them.

I had an aunt, my mother's sister who enjoyed making biscuits. And she made biscuits every day for her husband and for anybody who was visiting at that moment, she even made biscuits for her little dog. But nobody could match Aunt Mary's biscuits in town. Now don't ask me what she did to them, or how she made them, and how many things she put in them. She had her unique style of cooking biscuits, and that's an imitation of how God made us. He made us from the same dust of the Earth. From the dust of the Earth He scooped the clay by the banks of the river He kneeled Him down, molding man in His image, and into him He blew the breath of life and man became a living soul. And God said, Amen, Amen.

Uniquely different. Men are uniquely different. No one in the world can play your part. Do you know your part? Do you know what God has made of you? Do you know the qualities that He's placed in you and the opportunities He's given you to be that unique person that He molded and shaped. Nobody in this world can play your part. Ain't no sense in you talking bout I can't do this, and I can't do that, I'm not good as her, I'm not good as him. Ain't no sense in even saying it! God made you a unique person, and gave you the unique qualities to do what He's called on you to be and to do, and nobody in the world can play your part.

No one can make your contribution to the body of Christ but you. No one that you've met, no one that you've made friends of, nobody in the family can do what God has called you out to do, but you. All abilities come from God, and God gave them at birth. Did you hear what the psalmist said? He said at one point, for there is not a word in my tongue that O Lord, Thou knowest it altogether. And then he went on to say that, for thou hast possessed my reins: thou hast covered me in my mother's womb. Sometimes a mother has more than one child. My mother had nine, but every one of them even though we were born the next of kin came out with a uniqueness of their own, and it cannot be measured or matched by anybody else in the house. He gave it to us at birth.

Studies have shown that the average person possesses from 500-700 abilities, and that's an amazing array of skills. Think about yourself. Did you realize you had that many abilities wrapped up in you? Did you know all the things that God put in your life, and qualified you to do? Aw, come on, have you tried any of them? If you didn't try but one to show off, you got enough sense to do a lot of things, and you ought to be about the business of doing it.

The study shows that a brain can store one hundred million facts. And you thought that this computer was the only thing you could work with. God gave us the ability, and the mind, the brain to store all of these qualities and possibilities, and all we have to do is use what He has given us, and be whatever it is He desired, and what He's called us to be. The study also showed the mind can handle 15,000 decisions a second. What? 15,000 decisions a second, and you think this computer here in front of me is good! No, God put that computer in my brain a long time ago and He has matched it in yours. This study shows that your nose can smell up to 10,000 different odors, and you can know the difference in what you're smelling. It also showed that your touch can detect an item one twenty five thousandth of an inch thick. Just your touch! God made us unique individuals. It also shows that your tongue can taste one part of quinine in two million parts of water. Can you imagine that? He has made us so sensitive and our minds so sharp that we can taste quinine in two million parts of water. You are born with incredible abilities, an amazing creation of God.

Part of the church's responsibility is to identify and release your ability for serving God. So what if you just come to church and look good; God has called us to carry His message to a dying world, and to show the world that He has the power to make of this world and individuals what He chooses to make of it. Every ability that you have can be used to serve God. I was looking in the Bible for some pointers in terms of abilities that's been mentioned, and the Bible speaks of a number of them, I just jotted a few of them. It talks about artistic abilities. The Bible teaches us that we have the Architectural sense to design buildings, and to design whatever it is we choose to design. And that you can use that ability not just to design buildings, but to design in other people. It talks about the ability to administrate -- to be in charge of what God wants us to do.

God called Moses to the mountain and said to him, 'I want you to go down to Pharaoh's house and tell Pharaoh to let My people go.' Moses said, 'Lord, I can't do that. I've just been driven out of the Kingdom, and I've been told not to show up again. I wish you wouldn't assign me to do that.' God said, I want you to go and tell Pharaoh to let My people go. And Moses thought, what can I tell Him, what excuse can I give Him that He'd just leave me alone. Moses said, Lord I'm tied tongue. I can't even talk straight. When I go down to the Kingdom, and see Pharaoh and people come from all kingdoms, and all places of the world to pay homage to the King, What shall I say?, and who shall I say sent me? God told him, 'just tell Pharaoh, I am that I am sent you.' Well, if Moses can go down to carry that message to a King, then God can affect the delivery of people in bondage. He is somebody who uses a part of their creative mind that He's placed in him to go carry out His Word.

I look over in the book and there are people who are great thinkers. They found a lot of the things that were edible and became great cooks of their time. But they all used the mental capacity God had given them to learn what was needed and do what they knew to do. There were candy makers and rug makers, and designers. There were embalmers, engravers, gardeners, leading people in all kinds of management; masonry, music, teaching. God has a place in church where your talents can serve.

When God made men, He designed him in a way that whatever God needs, He's already put it on this earth, and you never know what God is calling you out to do in this world, and it's no sense in trying to tell him, Lord I don't know how. What you should be doing is asking Him, Lord, teach me to know how to do it.

Church, look at the 139th Psalm, and look at what the Psalmist said to God. He said, whither shall I go from thy spirit? Or whither shall I flee from thy presence? If I ascend up into heaven, thou art there and if I mess around and make my bed in hell, behold, thou art there. If I take the wings of the morning, and dwell in the uttermost parts of the sea; even there shall thy hand lead me, and thy right hand shall hold me. If I say, surely the darkness shall cover me; even the night shall be light about me. Yea, the darkness hideth not from thee; but the night shineth as the day: the darkness and the light are both alike to thee. For thou hast possessed my reins: thou hast covered me in my mother's womb. I will praise thee; for I am fearfully and wonderfully made: marvelous are thy works; and that my soul knoweth right well.

God Bless You

The Marks of Jesus

"From henceforth let no man trouble me: for I bear in my body the marks of the Lord Jesus." Galatians 6:17

✝ The Marks of Jesus

"Let me share with you a scripture from the book of Galatians in the New Testament. I want to read some verses from chapter 6, I'm going to skip over a few I want to read from 7-10 and drop down to 17 as the basis for a message: Be not deceived; God is not mocked: for whatsoever a man soweth, that shall he also reap. For he that soweth to his flesh shall of the flesh reap corruption; but he that soweth to the Spirit shall of the Spirit reap life everlasting. And let us not be weary in well doing: for in due season we shall reap, if we faint not. From henceforth let no man trouble me: for I bear in my body the marks of the Lord Jesus." (KJV)

And that's what I want to talk about for a few minutes today, The Marks of Jesus. From henceforth let no man trouble me for I bear in my body the marks of the Lord Jesus. This is one of those interesting stories of the Apostle Paul as he wrote his 13 Epistles to the Christian church in his ministerial life after being called from a life of destruction if you will. Paul decided early in his life that he was going to have nothing to do with that church business. Wasn't gone have anything to do with Jesus Christ. He had made a life for himself. He was highly positioned in his career. He had stars and stripes to wear on his body, and a parade of soldiers following him around, and protecting him from the on slot of others. And then one day the Lord stopped him on his way to Damascus to destroy a church that had been created at Damascus, and the Lord spoke to Paul from his horse, and he said I looked and I saw a light brighter than the sun. And I heard a voice say to me, "*Saul, Saul, why persecuteth thou me?*" Is it hard to kick against the prick?

Well Paul's upbringing had already sounded alarms in his life because he was well versed in Jewish law, and he knew what God had declared on behalf of his nation and what God was doing for him in spite of all the turmoil in the land. So, instead of Paul trying to question that voice and out maneuver that Sun, he said I fell off my horse to the ground, and asked Him, Lord what will you have me do?

And the Lord told him, I want you to go on where you're going. I want you to go on to Damascus, but your mission will change on your way, and your name is being changed right now. You will no longer be called Saul, you will be called Paul. And then when Paul finished his tour of duty; Got to the journey as an old man, preaching and teaching the word of God, Paul is now saying to the Galatian church that from henceforth let no man trouble me, for I bear in my body the marks of Jesus Christ.

When he wrote this message to the Galatian church Paul had grown old. He was going to his not retiring years, but the finishing of his course and as he traveled and remembered and fought on his way he saw himself stamped with the marks of Jesus. And one would wonder what he could be talking about when he talks about the marks of Jesus.

He had grown to the point where he had been wounded by conflict. All of his ministerial life he had attempted to follow the scriptures as Jesus taught them, and he had decided that he would run the race. But he discovered that at the end of his journey, he had been tortured, beaten and bruised and wounded in the battle for salvation and he could see himself in the same place with the wounds of Jesus Christ who died on a cross, crying out, Father, forgive them for they know not what they do. Who asked for help for dying men, women, and gave of his all to save dying humanity. And now Paul is saying, I have the wounds of conflict.

Furrows are now on his face. When you get a certain age, time start to catch up with you. You don't look like that pretty picture you once looked at and admired every day when you got up and looked on the dresser and then looked in the mirror at yourself. Paul says time was catching up with him, and he could see and feel the furrows on his face. Then he looked, and saw, and felt the change in his life... Not that spry, energetic young man that was riding that horse one day and attempting to destroy God's house, God's people, God's church. He had given his life for the cause and had gone all the way to life's end and he could see the furrows now on his face. He saw fear of change coming to the point that he had no way of determining what tomorrow would bring. And so He had to just accept what was given to him on a day to day basis.

But he also saw Himself as in service to His Master. He gave up the things he had dreamed of, and had an affection for. Paul said that he's going to forget those things which are behind, look forth to those things which are before, and press toward the mark. But when he looked at himself, stamped with marks of life, wounded in conflict, furrows of years on his face from the change in his life in the service of the Master. He said I bear branded on my body the marks of Jesus.

The branding was a mark of shame. He remembered that the world crucified Christ on a cross; nails in His hands, spikes in His feet. They abused Him, and beat and scorned Him, and nothing could be done about it. They put a security guard at His grave to be sure that nobody moved His body and pretended that He had risen as He said He would. But Sunday morning, He got up out of that grave and Paul is now saying, I bear branded on my body the marks of Jesus.

No man was branded of his own free will. Nobody wanted to be a slave. Nobody wanted to carry somebody's branding mark and name them according to the owner of the human being. Paul saw himself as one of those people who should have known better than to handle Jesus like that, but he found himself following Him before it was all over, and now he sees himself branded with the marks of Jesus. Paul hadn't planned on becoming the filth of the world. I said at the beginning of this message, he had already achieved high marks, he was already well positioned in his profession in life. So why would he want to become a slave to another cause that he even disagreed with? God didn't make him a slave he made him a servant and that was to carry out His will, and to carry His word to a dying world.

Paul had never dreamed of the loss of his home. And having to sleep and live wherever somebody was nice enough to give him a night's rest; to live so much time on boats and ships going from one city, and one place to another, having to preach the gospel of Jesus Christ. No home of his own.

Look at the comparison to Jesus. Jesus said to His disciples one day when a man was saying, Jesus, I want to go with you. I want to be where you are. I want to do what you're doing. I love your style. Jesus said let me explain something to you, "The foxes have holes, the birds of the air have nests, but the Son of man hath nowhere to lay His head." And so Paul found himself in that position where he had no home to go to, he had nowhere to lay his head, except the kindness of the people he served.

No family. He couldn't go home at night, and just go to rest and get back up early in the morning, and go back to work. He had to travel the universe on behalf of God. And if you don't have family close, how can you depend on friends? But everywhere He went, He had to find Him some friends, to help bear Him up and carry the load. He hadn't planned on a life of privation. Being alone so much. Being by Himself with the wisdom and knowledge, and understanding He had, and all of the work He had done, Paul found himself in some strange predicaments, and at the very end of his life he said to Timothy, one of his young ministers, he wrote him a note and sent it down through the chain and said to him, I want you to come see me. I need you to bring me a coat, stop at Troas and pick it up for me, it's cold in the dungeon. And I want you as you travel, be careful of the enemies out there, Alexander did me much harm. And I want you to understand that you have to walk around the problem spots and the problem areas, and keep yourself as strong as you can. Now, don't worry about me. If you can't get here in time, to bring me that coat from Troas while I'm in the dungeon at Rome, I want you to know I have finished my course. I fought a good fight, and I'm willing now to be reckoned to my kingdom, to go to my God so don't you worry if you can't get here.

Paul didn't choose it. Paul didn't pick out this profession. I said to you at the beginning, Paul got knocked down by God, off of his horse, and Paul said I didn't choose it. Necessity is laid upon me. Yes, woe unto me if I preach not the gospel, for if I do this thing willingly I have a reward.

Look at the marks of Jesus – Jesus had two kinds of marks. He had outward marks, and then inward marks. The first mark we can declare as one of God's choosing for His Son, and for the rest of us who claim a relationship with Him is self-denial. We have to give up self. We cannot just pretend that everything is for me, and mine, and the things that I want for myself. We have to give up a number of things in our lives just to be on the right page with Jesus Christ. And so Jesus denied himself. If any man will come after me, he must deny himself.

Then another outward mark is the mark of prayer. The prayer life. A lot of people don't want to hear about no prayer life. Don't want to pray about nothing, don't believe in prayer. But everything Jesus believed in, everything He taught started with prayer. "Father forgive them for they know not what they do." He went out in the wilderness and prayed forty days and forty nights just praying to God to guide Him and keep Him and keep Him strong enough to carry out His will. And every time He got ready to move, He prayed!

One day His disciples came to Him and said, "Master, teach us to pray." They had watched Him so much, and He got so much result. Every time He prayed, God answered. And His disciples said to Him, "Master, teach us to pray." Jesus said when you pray, first of all don't do as the hypocrites do. Don't pray standing in the streets, at the corner, so that you can be heard of men. Enter into your closet, in the chamber of your soul, go in, and when you shut the door, pray in secret, for what the Lord hears in secret He will reward you openly. So now when you pray, you start by saying, *"Our Father- He's not just yours, He is everybody's Father, so you pray, Our Father, who art in heaven, Hallowed be Thy name, Thy kingdom come, Thy will be done, on earth as it is in heaven."* He said, you've got to have a prayer life.

You know every one of us present here, and everyone present listening to me can recognize that you didn't make it this far on your prayer only. Somebody prayed for you, and they went down in secret prayer, and they prayed for you when you had no knowledge of their prayers, you didn't know what they were asking God to do for you. You just got the result. And so we like to, every now and then say, mama prayed. Mama prayed, but a whole lotta other folk in the community prayed also, that you would survive the onslaught of the things happening in your life. So, you've got to have a prayer life. Pray in the morning, pray at noon, pray all day long, pray! God is with you everywhere that you go and He can take care of your situation.

Love for your fellowman is a third inward mark of Jesus. You can't just be in love with yourself. You can't just do everything for your own self. There are people out there crying, "Somebody care about me! Somebody love me! Somebody touch my life, and let me live a better existence!" Jesus had this outward mark, and Paul saw that, and Paul spent his life following the construct of Jesus when Jesus called him and sent him on a new mission

And then there is a spiritual mark that is inherent in Jesus, and Paul adopted that mark. The true marks of Jesus are not the outward, but inward. I said the true marks of Jesus are not the outward, but inward. If any man hath not the spirit of Christ he's none of His. Look at the three spiritual marks of Jesus.

First of all, there's the mark of obedience. Whosoever shall do the will of God, the same is my brother, and sister, and mother. One day Jesus was in a crowd, and somebody asked Him to point out His mother to them, and look at this strange answer Jesus gave, "Whosoever shall do the will of God, the same is my brother, and sister, and mother." Here is Jesus claiming all of us. No matter where we're from, no matter where we are in life, no matter how far we think we are going, Jesus has the audacity to claim all of us. To claim us as a brother. To claim us as a sister, to claim us a mother. You can't beat a relationship like that – can you?

The second spiritual mark that I want to point out is the mark of love. By this shall all men know that ye are my disciples, if you have love one to another. You can be a disciple of Jesus Christ if you've got love for other folk. Love is not selfish, it's kind. And Jesus came to show us how to love. To love our enemies, to love our friends, to love our families, to love our extended families, to love people in general. Love … love … Jesus says.

Finally, the spiritual mark of sacrifice. If any man would come after me let him deny himself and take up his cross and follow me. I want to say that one more time. This is the mark of Jesus, the mark of sacrifice. If any man would come after me, let him deny himself, and take up his cross and follow me. At the cross, at the cross, where I first saw the light, and the burden of my heart, rolled away. It was there by faith, I received my sight, and now I am happy all the day!

Church, wherever you are at this moment and can hear me speak let me just ask you one final question. The conclusion of this matter ought to make you come down to the point where you can say, I have seen the marks of Jesus. Can He see mine? I have seen the marks of Jesus. Can Jesus see mine?

God Bless You

Toiling All Night and Taking Nothing

"And Simon answering said unto him, Master, we have toiled all the night, and have taken nothing: nevertheless at thy word I will let down the net." Luke 5:5

✝ Toiling All Night and Taking Nothing

Let me share with a scripture from the gospel of Luke fifth chapter, and I want to read several verses of that chapter in your hearing:

"And it came to pass, that, as the people pressed upon him to hear the word of God, he stood by the lake of Gennesaret, And saw two ships standing by the lake: but the fishermen were gone out of them, and were washing their nets. And he entered into one of the ships, which was Simon's, and prayed him that he would thrust out a little from the land. And he sat down, and taught the people out of the ship. Now when he had left speaking, he said unto Simon, Launch out into the deep, and let down your nets for a draught. And Simon answering said unto him, Master, we have toiled all the night, and have taken nothing: nevertheless at thy word I will let down the net. And when they had this done, they enclosed a great multitude of fishes: and their net brake. And they beckoned unto their partners, which were in the other ship, that they should come and help them. And they came, and filled both the ships, so that they began to sink. When Simon Peter saw it, he fell down at Jesus' knees, saying, Depart from me; for I am a sinful

man, O Lord. For he was astonished, and all that were with him, at the draught of the fishes which they had taken: (KJV)

I want to talk for a few minutes from this central theme, "Toiling All Night, and Taking Nothing." "Toiling All Night and Taking Nothing." This passage is an encouragement to those who have been laboring but without success, the success that they hoped for. Look at the story here of how Jesus came on the scene for this particular episode.

Jesus was already preaching and teaching. The people in the surrounding areas had called Him from one place to another. They had watched Him perform miracles both on top of mountains, and in valleys and by the waterside. Jesus had finished healing a number of people for their individual ailments and diseases. Everybody who came to Him, He touched them- and healed their bodies, minds, and spirits, and gave them a new charge to keep. Out there on the lake Jesus had been preaching all day, and He needed a little time to Himself, and so the crowd just kept growing cause they wanted to hear what this man of God had to say. And they crowded Him until finally, He went down to the lakes edge, and these two boats were parked there or docked there; and their owners had gone out of the boats, they were now empty. And Jesus prevailed with Simon to let Him sit on his boat and finish teaching the people. And so he agreed to let Him sit on that boat, and he kind of launched it out a little bit in the water so that He would be outside of stepping distance from the crowd, and Jesus kept preaching and teaching the Word of God.

And when He had finished that sermon, that message to the people, He said to Simon, now I want you to launch out in the deep, and I want you to catch some fish. Simon said to Him, Master, we have fished all night and caught nothing. But if you want me to go out into the deep I'll do it. And so his partners got on that boat and launched out a little ways and Jesus said to him, "Now let down your net for a draw." And he said they let the net down and it was so many fishes crowding that net, the net broke. They had to call for back-up. So they called the partners from the other boat and told them, you need to come here. We've got something over here that you want to see. And they got in their boat and went and both boats were filled to capacity to the point where the boat almost sank. Peter said, "Master this is too much for me." His name is Simon Peter. Simon said, "this is too much for me. We have been here all night long and caught nothing. And here you tell us to simply let down the net for a draw and we can't haul what we've caught."

There are those of us who can relate to this story. When Simon said to Christ, we have toiled all night, and taken nothing. Look at our lives. Look at where we have come from, where we are. Look at the families we came from; our mothers, fathers, and grandparents who worked a lifetime just trying to achieve a normal living. And every time they almost made it, something happened, and they couldn't get there for what they came for. And so we look at ourselves even in church life. We see ourselves toiling year after year, all of our lives, and then coming to the point where we have to declare, I have fished all night and caught nothing.

There are those of us who are pastors, who pastor churches for a lifetime, giving up everything we can find to give up. Struggling against the tide, suffering for the cause of humanity just as Jesus taught us to do. And then grow old believing that, I've spent my whole life and not achieved what I set out to achieve. Fished all night and caught nothing.

There are those members of the church and members of the Christian community who have taught in the classrooms, in the Sunday School, everything they could touch to give people the best of chances, and wonder sometimes as they go to the end of the journey, what have I achieved?, who have I helped? Did I simply waste a life and not gain one? I have fished all night and caught nothing. Weeks go by, months go by. Years go by, and the toiling just keeps on going. In my life somebody said, "I've had my share of trouble, but the darkest hour is just before day."

There are those who give of themselves, make the sacrifices, missionaries on the field, suffering against the tides of time, the world's order, give up a whole life and then at the end wonder, why have I fished all night and caught nothing? Hope diminishes, disappointments come. You give all you've got, you sacrifice all you can, and yet in the end hopelessness takes over. Jesus saw the condition of the fisherman. Can you imagine while He's preaching and teaching from the water's edge, to the people standing on the river's edge, and the beach and all of that, just filled the area to hear what He's got to say. And yet when it came to a point where the crowd had grown so large that he could not get over to let them hear what He's saying, He said to the fisherman, "let me sit on your boat, and I want you to just launch out just a little bit, and let me finish what I'm doing." And they allowed Him to do it.

There's nothing wrong with allowing Jesus in your life to do what you need to do in the cause of Christianity and humanity. And so He sat there and preached and taught until it was time to reward them for their dedication to the cause, for allowing Him to use their boats, and showed them that not only can He heal the sick, not only can He speak peace to troubled minds, not only can He brings families back together, He can still reward you with impossibilities. Cast your net for a draw. He didn't say, go back fishing. He didn't say try it again. He said cast your nets for a draw, and the fish heard, and filled the net. Don't you tell me this Christ we serve, this God we serve cannot do the impossible, and He will do what no other man can do!

The command to continue under disappointment and apparent defeat bears frequently, enters the thoughts of abandonment. When the thoughts of abandonment come, your declaration is I cannot go any further. That's when Christ really wants to see you. When you admit you cannot go any further, He says, "I will be your friend that sticks closer than a brother." When He hears you say it's too hard; He says, "My yolk is easy, and my burden is light." Don't you ever believe that life can meet out to you hard things that you cannot handle if Christ is with you! So He says don't you say it's too hard. I can handle it. And don't you declare it's too long of a journey. The Lord says toil on and faint not.

The spirit and acts of obedience: At Thy word, I will let down the net. Those fishermen said, "Lord, we're declaring that we've done our best all night. We've used up the resources. We've stood the test of time because we're still here on the riverfront. But we've gone and washed our nets because we've caught nothing and we've labored all night. At Thou word, Simon said, I will let down my net." You can't beat that can you? All you need to do is listen to the Word of Christ. If He tells you to go, He's going with you. If He tells you to wait, He's waiting with you. "They that wait on the Lord shall renew their strength, they shall mount up with wings as eagles, run and not be weary, they shall walk and not faint." I will continue at my post. Simon says. In a word I fished all night and caught nothing. I've cleaned up my nets getting ready for another day. You asked me to put my net down, and I'm gonna follow your word. And I know if you tell me to do it, you're capable of making it happen. I will let down my net for a draw. I will continue my post.

How many times have you decided and declared, I've had enough of this. I'm giving it up? I am not going to waste any more of my time trying to do the impossible, and yet it's just past that period and that point that your blessing is waiting. If Simon had said, I am not going to let down my net, he would have gone home empty again. If he had said, Lord , I doubt that I'll be successful by doing what you told me to do, but I'll do it anyway he would have gone home without a draw.

But Jesus said let down your net for a draw, and He said it at the point where hope had passed. If it is necessary to change my methods, I'll do it.

Let me talk about the large reward and I'm gone. After much labor and suffering dedication, God will say to us, I know your work, I know your labor. I know that you have been faithful over these things, I got blessings for you for more than that. There is a reward for working on till the battle is won. You know I said to my wife this morning when we were getting dressed; we like to complain about how long freedom takes, how long we have to suffer before something good happens to us. But I told her you have to remember, Jesus came over forty-two generations ago.

God promised deliverance to Israel, but Jesus came forty-two generations later to save the world. Don't you tell me God forgot, that He doesn't remember what He promised, that He can't deliver on His promises. No, don't you tell me that God will forget. Just keep on in your prayer life. Hear my prayer oh Lord. Pray daily, pray every day, pray all the time. God will answer your prayer. He may not come when you want Him, but He's on time.

Wailing and waiting. Keep on shedding tears, keep on crying but wait on the Lord. You may go forth weeping, but we shall come forth rejoicing. In a way we did not expect it. No way in the world Simon and them ever believed that all they had to do was listen to Jesus, and they would catch some fish. But they caught more than they could handle. One soweth, another reapeth. Church, if you believe in your heart that you should give it up because you've been toiling all night and caught nothing, don't give it up, don't quit, let Jesus guide you, and He will give you the draw.

God Bless You

Human Wreckage

"Holding faith, and a good conscience; which some having put away concerning faith have made shipwreck." I Timothy 1:19

† Human Wreckage

Our scripture comes from I Timothy of the New Testament. I want to take you to chapter one and read two verses in your hearing, verses 18 and 19, and I will take the message basically from verse 19:

"This charge I commit unto thee, son Timothy, according to the prophecies which went before on thee, that thou by them mightest war a good warfare; Holding faith, and a good conscience; which some having put away concerning faith have made shipwreck." (KJV)

I want to talk about Human Wreckage. Holding faith and a good conscience; which some having put away concerning faith have made shipwreck. Paul is an interesting fellow, he served a long spiritual life building the church of God traveling long distances to get to his assignment. In his day he spent a lot of time on ships traveling from one place to another and he discovered so many things about ship travel. How much danger you could be in going from one destination to another, and no matter how good the feeling at the beginning of a voyage, anything could go wrong along the way and you would be a helpless creature on the waters.

And so for this message for this writing to Timothy, his son in the ministry, Paul used a beautiful vessel at sea destroyed by storm or wreck to describe a broken life. He was teaching and preaching the word of God. And the word of God led him to the conclusion that the only thing God was concerned about really was our soul, and that if we didn't watch it, there were things that could destroy our balance, and destroy our relationship with Him; and Paul compared that relationship of man as it breaks along the way to that of a broken ship.

Paul associated a broken character with a loss of faith. Think about it; we are called upon to have faith in God, to allow Him in our lives, in our existence, to make those decisions that's critical to our existence, and our ending, if you will. It requires real character in faith, faith in God. Faith in one who is able to keep us from falling, and who can present us faultless before His throne. He said, "Holding faith and a good conscience which some have put away have made shipwreck."

I remember just recently having the opportunity for another time, I've watched it so many times over the past years, the story of the Titanic, the ship that was celebrated as it made its voyage. And when it got ready to leave shore it was declared as an indestructible vessel, that nothing could sink that ship. It was celebrated with all of the fanfare, the beauty that could go with the creation of something that magnificent. It carried as a load people who were higher class, who had wealth, who had position in life because they wanted to make the maiden voyage of the Titanic. And so when they pushed off from shore, it had all of the fanfare that one could ever dream of, and people were standing, waving in the distance as she set sail to sea. You can imagine, and you saw it yourself, you can imagine the feeling of grandeur that a person or persons would have on something that magnificent, built with such pride, and built so expensively that man could declare it is impossible to sink it.

And so they set sail. Paul would equate that Titanic ship with all of that beauty; flags flying being ready for sail. People at the bar having a good time. People walking around getting ready to really enjoy the trip. Paul would suggest that that's how you could look at a voyage as a young person. When you have already boarded the ship of life with no relationship with God, you don't know who owns the universe, or who sustains you in life. And so you set sail with all of the beauty and grandeur of life and nature and somewhere along that journey life takes a downward turn.

So many of our young have started out with such beauty, such a desire for life and all that it had to offer. So much aspiration and inspiration to make this voyage in life become successful and be able to proclaim, "I've been there and done that!" Somehow along the way we recognized that voyage was more than we were ready for. And so somewhere along the way we lost our way because we did not have stability in God. And so we traveled, we had fun, and there along the way we recognized that life was turning sour, and young people lost their way in so many places and in so many ways that they couldn't find a way back.

So sometimes in life, your ship runs aground at a young age. It was possible for the Titanic to never get into deep waters, because during the celebration they could have not guided the ship in such a way that it would leave the shore. It would simply embed itself in shallow ground, in shallow waters. But like a young person, it was not stopped in shallow waters. It was taken out into the depths of the ocean.

Sometimes in life your voyage is disrupted, not in your youth, not in your young tender years, but it waits until you get into midlife. And you believe that all that you've ever dreamed of is in your sight. You believe that whatever you want, you're in a position to get. And it makes no difference what life is meeting out right now, you believe you can overcome it with just where you are in life at the moment.

That's what they felt on the Titanic. It had gotten out in mid waters. And it was such a celebration that they failed to watch where they were going. And not only where they were going, but what in life was coming after this. And then one moment they looked up and there was this great iceberg, bearing down upon this magnificent ship, and it was no way to turn it and bypass the ice. When you get into mid-life, if you don't watch yourself, you can forget to watch what's coming at you, what's already around you, and you will find yourself in a position where you cannot turn and go another direction, and be safe on your journey.

Hundreds of people died in that ocean because a ship had been declared impossible to sink and nothing could stop it until it was too late for them to realize what was coming towards them was bigger than what they had going in their direction.

And so the iceberg hit the Titanic and that beautiful ship took its own time and destroyed those on it, those who could swim. Paul once said he was on a boat and he got almost to where he was supposed to get, and a storm came up. And said the men who were steering the ship, carrying him as a prisoner, a spiritual prisoner to Rome say they fought with that water, they fought with that storm as long as they could and then the ship was going in such a direction that even Paul, the prisoner had to say to them, "Don't worry too much about it, just keep working at it all of you will survive." Now he didn't go so far as to say because I'm on here, but God was with him. And he said to those people you will survive. And he said that ship tossed and turned, and it broke up in the waters. Paul said to these people who were steering the ship here's what I advise you to do. I want those of you who can swim to pick broken pieces of the vessel and swim to shore. The shore is right over there. But those of you who can, hold on, you will not be killed in this storm, you will survive. And they went on to shore in the middle of that storm but they had God with them. Keep in mind I'm talking about that Titanic that was not supposed to sink, It could not sink, and it did sink.

Too many folk have left God behind and decided to take a voyage of their own choosing in their own minds. But if God is with you in the storm, you will survive. If God is with you in the midst of the waters and an iceberg is coming, God can float you in another direction. And so sometimes it's not only in your youth, that you may run aground, and become shipwrecked. Sometimes it's in midlife when everything is going well and everything is going your way. You have no way of knowing what tomorrow will bring.

Shipwrecked sometimes comes at the close of a voyage. You can either have a shipwreck at the beginning of that voyage running aground or out there in the midst of the ocean a storm can take control or even in old age you can be taken down because you have lost your way along the way. In other words you done got almost home and decided that you can make it on your own now. Somebody statistically proved that most of your fatal accidents on the highway come within twenty-five miles of your home. You can travel all over the world and come and relax so much that it causes you to lose control of the very car that you're driving, and you don't feel that you're in any danger because you are in your territory. You're almost home.

People who have served God a lifetime, who have given Him their dedication along the way get to the point in old age where they say, "I've done enough, I ain't gone do no more." And they can lose themselves in that voyage of life almost home. They can see land in sight, but the watch has not been kept.

I urge those of you who've been victimized by a pandemic; if you are not able to leave your house and go to church, I advise you not to lose your faith in God. You're almost home, and you don't want to just say, I don't need the church anymore. In life we may have everything we need, but at the end of the journey we may go to sleep.

Shipwrecked affects the very highest element of our being. And this is what I want to close with. Shipwrecked affects the highest element of our being, and that is our conscience. A good conscience is the sweetest meat to which ever a man sat down to eat, or the grandest music one will ever play. Good conscience, good conscience will tell you whether you are young, middle aged, or old; "A charge to keep I have, a God to glorify. Who gave His Son my soul to save, and fit it for the sky. Help me to watch and pray, and on thyself rely by faith assured I will obey for I shall never die."

Good conscience is cleansed by the blood of Christ. In order to have a good conscience cleansed by the Word of Christ you've got to have it enlightened by God's Word. Now Christ came to teach us the way, and to teach us God's Word and God's will. In order for me to have a good conscience in the first place, God has got to cleanse it! God's Word has to give me enlightenment, and it can only be quickened by the Holy Spirit. The three persons of the Godhead are having something to do with us every day. God the Father, God the Son, and God the Holy Spirit.

Finally, let me just share this with you. A good conscience is something that wealth cannot purchase. A good conscience is something that envy cannot steal. A good conscience is something that poverty cannot harm. A good conscience is something sin cannot strip from its crown. Wreck a good conscience, and all is lost. Let me say that again. We're talking about being shipwrecked. And life can be like a ship "wrecked". You wreck a good conscience and all is lost.

God Bless You!

Ask What Shall I Give Thee

"In that night did God appear unto Solomon, and said unto him, Ask what I shall give thee." 2 Chronicles 1:7

✝ Ask What I Shall I Give Thee

Let me make this observation before I go into the message to share with you why I am dressed in this garb, along with the cap. I'm seeking to honor today's message to graduates across the nation: high school, college, technical school, wherever it is you're graduating from. I want to say congratulations and Godspeed to you. I make no apologies, they're not mine to give in terms of everything being out of order where we normally would have our Baccalaureate sermons, and commencement exercises where people get a chance to gather in large audiences and celebrate their achievements. There are so many of you out there today who cannot do that today. But we want to just share with you a message that may be of benefit to the graduates of 2020.

I ask those of you who are listening online to please share this message with someone that's graduating from school, and feels a sense of loss because they've not been able to do a grand celebration or grand march. So it's up to us to share our blessings.

I want to talk today with you from 2 Chronicles the first chapter and I want to read the 6th through the twelfth verses:

"And Solomon went up thither to the brasen altar before the LORD, which was at the tabernacle of the congregation, and offered a thousand burnt offerings upon it. In that night did God appear unto Solomon, and said unto him, Ask what I shall give thee. And Solomon said unto God, Thou hast shewed great mercy unto David my father, and hast made me to reign in his stead. Now, O LORD God, let thy promise unto David my father be established: for thou hast made me king over a people like the dust of the earth in multitude. Give me now wisdom and knowledge, that I may go out and come in before this people: for who can judge this thy people, that is so great? And God said to Solomon, Because this was in thine heart, and thou hast not asked riches, wealth, or honour, nor the life of thine enemies, neither yet hast asked long life; but hast asked wisdom and knowledge for thyself, that thou mayest judge my people, over whom I have made thee king: Wisdom and knowledge is granted unto thee; and I will give thee riches, and wealth, and honour, such as none of the kings have had that have been before thee, neither shall there any after thee have the like." (KJV)

Let me talk about "Ask What I Can Give Thee", and just so we can put this in a graduation order, I'm going to ask the organist if he would play a short Pomp and Circumstance for us. (Music played by Dr. George West)

"Ask What I Shall Give Thee." Solomon had already been crowned King in the absence of his father, David, very young and tender. He had been put into this fashion completely out of his league. Here is a nation of people that he has inherited, and he is to follow in the footsteps of his father David; who has been described as a man after God's own heart. And so, Solomon, as he grappled with how to, how will I make decisions for a nation so great, and how will I do it as successfully as my father did. But he went up to the temple in his usual fashion to give an offering to the Lord, and after the ceremony was over, he went home to rest for the night, and God showed something that we all need to recognize. That it makes no difference who you are, or where you are, God can find you, and have some questions to ask.

In his sleep that night in a dream, God spoke to him, and said Solomon, "What will you have me give you. As you graduate from College, as you graduate from high school, all of the places you have gone and sacrificed time and energy, learning trades and learning professions and learning all of the things you need to learn, and then coming to a point where you can't even enjoy it; something else is going on in the world that you can't stop, you can't hinder and you can't change. And so you have to live with it and deal with it. But you've already prepared yourself in whatever fashion you can to make a run for it. To live a successful journey in your life and now all of your plans have been torn asunder. Everything you thought was good with you, and you would be able to do under any set of circumstances are now gone the way of the wind.

That proves something in Solomon's words; that God can, and will find you under any circumstances, and He will have a word with you no matter what the condition. And so in his sleep, God asked him the question Solomon that is, "What will you ask me to give you?"

And look at how Solomon answered God. He said Thou hast shown great mercy to my father David. First of all he wanted God to know that he understands that God is able, and capable of doing what He wants to do, with any person alive, under any set of circumstances. He said to God in that dream, 'you've been good, you showed mercy to my father David, and then thou hast made me great in his stead. You put on the hearts of men that I was the successor of one the greatest Kings they ever had." So he would take that throne, and abide by the rules that his father had established. And He said to the Lord, Lord thou hast made me to reign in his stead. Thou hast made me king over a people like the dust of the earth in multitude. Lord you gave me a job so big, I can't even conceive of it, I can't even imagine being able to handle all of these things that you placed upon my heart, and in my hands.

God is too kind to His children and too great to give them gifts without having conditions which must be followed. God got a blessing for you. But whatever He blesses you with He got conditions to go with those blessings. And you've got to understand then when God bless you, you've got to be prepared to not only accept His blessing but you've got to give of yourself what He requires of you to give.

Shall I give you prosperity? Ask for it. But if you ask for prosperity you better know I've sent diligence, hard work, and struggle. You've got to give of yourself if you expect to have prosperity. You've got to be a civil minded person. You can't just have everything for yourself. You've got to be civil to others, you've got to be kind to your fellow man -- to love your fellowman as I have loved you. And so you must not only be hard working- you know when you look at what God is requiring of Solomon I guess you can put it in the vernacular of a mother raising her child. You know a mother doesn't work 8-5 to raise a child. She works from can to can't. There's no such thing as 8 hour, 10 hour, 12 hour days. It's all day and all night. And so when you look at it in that fashion, God is saying to Solomon, you've got to be diligent. You've got to stay on the job. When everybody else goes home, you've got to be there. When you think the job has been done, there's some more of it to do. and you've got to be civil, you've got to love what you're doing; you've got to love who you're doing it for.

And if you want to be prosperous, you've got to be faithful. Be faithful every day. Not some days, not sometimes, or when I can. You've got to be faithful all the time. God said to Solomon when asked "what shall I give you?" Solomon, let me ask you this, shall I give you human love. Ask for it.

But you better know you've got to be honorable as I give you human love. You've got to honor those others that you think you ought not to respect, but you've got to have honor to give if I give you human love. If a human being is going to love you, you've got to first love them. If you want human love, be virtuous. Stop claiming everything for yourself. You've got to give to others, and give because God has first given to you. And so if you ask for human love, it must be virtuous.

Nobody's asking you to be perfect but give from your heart, and do unto others what you would have them do unto you. If you ask me what I shall give you. Shall I give you knowledge? Ask for it. But if you want knowledge you've got to be studious. If you want knowledge you've got to find out something on your own. I hope too many of you didn't copy off somebody's paper to finish school. You need to know for yourself; you have to learn how to *rightly divide* the word of truth for yourself so if you want knowledge you've got to keep studying to shew thyself approved.

I'm gonna finish with this one. Shall I give you eternal life? Ask for it. But if you ask me for eternal life you've got to know you must be born again. You must be born in the spirit. Just being born in the flesh isn't sufficient. If you want eternal life then you must be born of the spirit of Jesus Christ. You must be born again. You must put down the old person and take on the new. This is what you are called upon to do as you go into the world and take your place in society. God is asking, "what will you have me give you?" And you are saying I want this, and that, and the other. If you want eternal life not only do you have to be born again, you have to have faith in Jesus Christ. " No one comes to the Father, except by me, Jesus said." If you want eternal life you've got to believe and trust Jesus Christ as your Savior and He will help you through. He will provide, He will make a way. And so I say to you in closing; Ask what I shall give thee God asks. Solomon answered, Lord. Wisdom and knowledge is granted unto thee. The Lord said this to Solomon:

"And God said to Solomon, Because this was in thine heart, and thou hast not asked riches, wealth, or honour, nor the life of thine enemies, neither yet hast asked long life; but hast asked wisdom and knowledge for thyself, that thou mayest judge my people, over whom I have made thee king: Now listen to what God said to him: Wisdom and knowledge is granted unto thee; and I will give thee riches, and wealth, and honour, such as none of the kings have had that have been before thee, neither shall there any after thee have the like."

If you ask God for wisdom and knowledge to know the difference between right and wrong, and to do that which is good and pleasing in His sight, and honor Him in the person of Jesus Christ as your Savior! He said I won't only give you what you ask me for, I'll give you all these other things.

Congratulations, and God Bless you for your journey into your world in a way you had not planned, but God has granted you the knowledge and wisdom to go forth.

God Bless You

Judging Prematurely

"Therefore judge nothing before the time, until the Lord come, who both will bring to light the hidden things of darkness, and will make manifest the counsels of the hearts: and then shall every man have praise of God." 1 Corinthians 4:5

† Judging Prematurely

Let me share with you a scripture from 1 Corinthians, Chapter 4. I'm going to concentrate on verse five but, I want read verses 1-5 in your hearing:

"Let a man so account for us, as of the ministers of Christ, and stewards of the mysteries of God. Moreover it is required in stewards, that a man be found faithful. But with me it is a very small thing that I should be judged of you, or of man's judgment: yea, I judge not mine own self. For I know nothing by myself; yet am I not hereby justified: but he that judgeth me is the Lord. Therefore judge nothing before the time, until the Lord come, who both will bring to light the hidden things of darkness, and will make manifest the counsels of the hearts: and then shall every man have praise of God." (KJV)

With that scripture I want to talk about judging prematurely. Paul is advising the Corinthian church or the church at Corinth about being so hasty in judging people, and he wanted to point out that his faithfulness to God requires him to not judge others, but He also is not even in a position to judge himself. And he says judge nothing till the Lord comes. Paul was thinking about his own work. Those of us who are students of the Bible, and have read a number of times the New Testament scriptures recognize how Paul was given his start when he had made his mind up to be his own man, to do things his own way, no matter who liked it or not, just do what he wanted to do himself, and God called him on it; stopped him and changed his mission by creating in him a new heart, and he could use the mind he had already refined to better serve the cause of God. So he was looking at his own work. It's one thing to have somebody tell you you've been faithful, but it's another for you to know you've been faithful. And Paul preached and taught, traveled from one place to another carrying God's word, all the way to the end of his life. And at the end of his life he could say with surety, I have fought a good fight, I've kept the faith. I finished my course.

But here at the church in Corinth, he was not only recognizing his own work, but he had carried with him the character that also lends itself to the work of God. And he knew he had been faithful to the word. Had attempted to develop the human spirit to God's liking. And so he knew his work was faithful, he knew his character was right. But he also had to look at the harsh treatments of others. Paul ran into some treacherous times. People who did him much harm. But here at the church in Corinth, he was not only recognizing his own work, but he had carried with him the character that also lends itself to the work of God. And he knew he had been faithful to the word. Had attempted to develop the human spirit to God's liking. And so he knew his work was faithful, he knew his character was right. But he also had to look at the harsh treatments of others. Paul ran into some treacherous times. People who did him much harm. Some of you remember me saying recently, when Paul was in the dungeon at Rome getting ready for his death he sent a letter to Timothy, his son in the ministry and said to him, I want you to come as soon as you can and bring me my coat. It's cold down here. And I want to get me some parchment, and bring that with you too. Parchment as you know, is the writing paper that Paul wrote his thirteen Epistles on and he had run out of writing materials and he said to Timothy, get me some parchment and bring it with you... Come as soon as you can. I know you got some problems trying to get here. I want you to know, I want you to watch out for Alexander- Alexander did me much harm. And if He would do it to me, He will do it to you. And then he finished his note to Timothy by saying, now if you don't get here don't let that worry you. Don't let that bother you. I have fought a good fight. I've kept the faith. I've finished my course.

And so while he was looking at his own work, checking over his own character, he also kept in mind the harsh treatment of others. But he knew he worked for Christ. And he worked only for Christs' approval here, and vindication in the hereafter. That, that's good, isn't it" Paul knew he was working for Christ here. But he was also working at his vindication in the hereafter. So we all know that we are here at church, and we are here to worship, wherever we are, we are here because we want God to recognize our trying, to recognize our spirit, our faith. But, also as He recognizes our faith, and our spirit, and our shortcomings in this life, we want Him to be a forgiving God, and see us through on the other side.

When the end comes, Paul is saying to the Corinthian people, I want you to know at that time what manner of man I am. So, I don't have to worry about you judging me now. I'm gonna keep on running this race, and running with patience. I'm gonna mount up with wings like eagles, run and not be weary. I'm going to walk and not faint. So you may not know who I am now, but when it's all over, you'll know whose I am.

I want you to recognize my pure motives. I try hard to lead you in the path of right and righteousness. I have no ulterior motives. Nothing negative in my mind towards you. I'm trying my best to show you how to get from here to yonder, and know who God is. You will know in the end when my life is over, my uprightness in conduct, and my faithfulness in witness. Judge nothing before its time. Observation is perpetually gathering facts. Some people don't like facts, they want stuff. One of the problems our great scientists is having right now, he's dealing with too many facts, and we want him to just stop giving facts, and give some fiction, so this mess will be over. And what he is saying is the more facts I gather, the more I have to work with and the more I tell you, you've got to watch what you are doing, the more you better believe it. Because I'm not dealing with fiction, I'm dealing with facts.

Turning facts over to reason. You see, reason looks at it by the law. Truth questions faith and opinion but right questions conduct. I want to say that again. We're going to turn facts over to reason. Reason looks at it by the law. Under reason truth comes in and truth questions faith and opinion. So you have got to stop using your opinion on everything. The truth comes by questioning faith, and opinion, but right questions conduct. What are you gonna do about it, and how are you gonna do it?

Reason decides the ability to reason. Don't judge before its time. Judging and revising judgment sometimes becomes necessary. Somebody said once two thirds of our statements turn out to be judgements. So you have to be careful about how you judge, and what you say about somebody, and how to feel about others, because if you talk too much, you've declared your judgment. And your judgment is not good. Judge nothing before its time.

You see, we all change from what we were to what we are now, we've changed. And if you keep on living, you're going to change again, and again, and again. Cause you didn't know what you were gonna be, we will all change. We change steadily. Every day of our life, we're changing. Not only in physical looks and sight. We're changing in heart, and mind, and understanding of the world about us, and what we thought yesterday won't cut it today; cause we are changing. We change by the years; from birth to death- we change. We don't recognize our change many times- it creeps upon us. And others can recognize our change much quicker than we can. But every year brings about a change.

Oh, you know who I'm talking about. I'm talking about you and me. The changing yearly, growing into a person you didn't even know to expect. And sometimes you wish you hadn't changed to what you got. We change in structure. Oh, you ain't your old fine self that you used to be! I don't care how much you try your best to lose the weight, to put it in another place and all that stuff, you're changing. Sometimes, no matter how hard you work at it, there ain't nothing you can do about it. Judge nothing before it's time. We're changing in intellect. Daily we learn new things. We learn how to rightly divide the word of truth over time. Intellectually, we are better at it today than we were yesterday. And if we keep on working at it, God will make us better tomorrow than we are today. Intellectually we're changing.

We're changing in spirit. You remember when the church didn't mean as much as it does now to you. See you can talk about the Pandemic all you want, and you glad to be getting some rest from the church, but you didn't want that much rest. Stay at home, don't go nowhere, don't enjoy the things you once enjoyed, don't eat out, don't sleep out. Don't do all the things you wish you could do. You've got to now change your habits, and your spirit changes in the process. Judge nothing before its time. Our perceptions change. What we think about something today is different than we thought about it yesterday. And it will be different tomorrow.

Scripture tells us, we grow in grace. Come up from a child growing in grace. And that's how a religion is supposed to deal with us. We are supposed to become more than we used to be. I'll tell you something else, even your taste changes. A lot of things you used to love, you can't stand no more. That's one of things I was looking at the conditions of the virus we got attacked by, and one of the things medical people tell us is that one of the main things you can look at and recognize is your loss of taste. Your taste changes. And it doesn't have to be in a tragic manner. It doesn't have to be a pandemic to make your taste change, you can change ordinarily because of time and circumstance. What you used to like, you don't like no more, who you used to like, you don't like no more. Your taste changes.

Our needs change. There was a time when we thought we just needed everything. Give me an armful, I need all of it. And then you discovered as you get older and more mature, that your needs are not as great as you thought they were. You can get along with a little of nothing. And you don't need all the stuff you thought you needed.

What seemed worthless at one stage of life in our history has become more valuable than at other times. You remember when there were some things going on in your life that you considered worthless-had no value to you. And you kept on living, and you kept on developing. And then you discovered that what you thought was worthless, is now valuable.

I had a friend in Louisville, Kentucky, Reverend E. Heard, who pastored a church with me in Mississippi and he went on to Kentucky and made good in his church work there. But he developed a hobby that he loved all of his life, but never had the time to do anything about it. And that was to restore old cars. And when I visited him, in fact I did a revival for him when I visited him, he had several old models of cars that he had restored to immaculate condition. And people from as far as California were searching him out to buy those old vintage cars. And he admitted that there was a time in his life when he just wanted a new one. He kept working hard just to get him a new one, a new car. And then he discovered the value was in the old one. And so he was restoring cars in his own yard that were more valuable than they were when they were brand new. And so we have to recognize that history provides us more value than a worthless young age. And we have to know that God is in the plan.

There's a lesson to young people in this message. Paul is here talking about judging nothing before its time. And some of our greatest judges are in the young people's category. In the first place, they are

Judging Prematurely

judgmental of people, period. You've been around a group when you were younger, that didn't like nobody. Everybody they met had a problem that they needed to fix, and nobody had it going on, but them. Young people judge methods of doing things. They want to get it done right now. Get out the way old folk, you take too long getting this project finished, getting it done. Let me have it. And then they realize that they don't even know how to fix it.

The methods of doing things, the facts of it, are lost in a haste to take control. Take charge. Did you know that the average young person never reaches the age of thirteen. They were looking forward to being 12 and then go straight from 12 to going on 14. Do you understand what I'm saying? They didn't want the next age to be mentioned, they wanted the age after that one to be mentioned. And so they went straight from 12 going on 14. And they never made another age limit until they got past 20. And then there was a time when they didn't to rush that age, they wanted to slow it down. I often wondered how come old folk couldn't remember the year they were born. Because they wanted to bring it back. Young folk couldn't remember the year they were born because they wanted to take it forward. But in each case we each want to judge the other. And Paul is saying judge nothing before its time.

We can be critical of that which does not come up in the useful standards. One of the things I truly hope we can achieve in this lifetime. We are going through a period of remembrance and celebration of some of our greatest civil rights leaders in this country. Right now brother Lewis is being carried through the circle. But wouldn't it be nice if we could somehow recognize a man's life before he dies. Wouldn't it be nice for others to learn what steps you took? What door did you open, how did you go about the task of bringing others into your circle? Instead of just judging what you think ought to have happened and still taking year after year after year to live, and redo the same things over.

Judge nothing before its time. Because you can do it prematurely, you can judge too early. See there's no way in the world for anybody to recognize the achievements of men and women in this world when they were young to the achievement they would've ultimately arrived at. And if we could've just bore with it. If we could've just hung on. We would have had a better opportunity to educate ourselves. Paul said, I'm not even in a position to judge myself. And so I'm gonna leave that up to God. I'm just gone to run on, and run this race and run it the best I can. I'm gonna keep the faith, and keep on struggling for the cause. And I'm going to expect Jesus to watch over me here on this earth, but He also promised me a home in glory. And so I want Him to watch me here, and take me there.

Judge nothing before its time.

God Bless You

Judging Prematurely

Life's Blessings

"Blessed is the man that walketh not in the counsel of the unGodly, nor standeth in the way of sinners, nor sitteth in the seat of the scornful." Psalm 1:1

✝ Life's Blessings

Let me share with you a scripture from the book of Psalms. It will be the first number of Psalms, and I want to share that Psalm with you in reading and then bring the message from a greater portion of it

"Blessed is the man that walketh not in the counsel of the unGodly, nor standeth in the way of sinners, nor sitteth in the seat of the scornful. But his delight is in the law of the Lord; and in his law doth he meditate day and night. And he shall be like a tree planted by the rivers of water, that bringeth forth his fruit in his season; his leaf also shall not wither; and whatsoever he doeth shall prosper. The ungodly are not so: but are like the chaff which the wind driveth away. Therefore the unGodly shall not stand in the judgment, nor sinners in the congregation of the righteous. For the Lord knoweth the way of the righteous: but the way of the unGodly shall perish." (KJV)

I want to talk a few minutes about "Life's Blessings." The first blessing I want to point out to you is the blessing of peace. One day Jesus was preaching out on the mountain and he came across a man who was demon possessed, and he had been tied out in the hills by his handlers because they couldn't subdue him, they couldn't do anything with him, nor could they do anything about his condition. But he had the mind that things would come and go. One day when he saw Jesus even in his demon possessed way out on the hillside he hollered out to Jesus, don't you pass me too, don't you do me like everybody else has done me. And Jesus said to him, what will you have me do? And he said, "Oh! if I could just be free of these demons in my life." And Jesus commanded that the demons would come out of him. And they requested, the demons did, for Jesus to send them into a herd of swine. Don't just abandon them, let them go into somebody else, something else. And Jesus allowed the demons to go into a herd of swine, and it was so many of them, it was so devastating that even the swine jumped into the ocean and drowned themselves. The man was found sitting comfortably at the feet of Jesus begging him, "master let me go with you, I don't want to go where I've been treated the way I've been treated, let me follow you. And Jesus told him no, I won't allow you to go with me. It's more problems out there that you're not prepared for, so I'm gonna let you go home and tell your friends how great things the Lord has done for you.

But the story goes that they found him sitting at the feet of Jesus, after the demons had been dismissed. One of the blessings of peace is that when you meet Jesus there is a calmness that comes over you. The things that bothered you so greatly, so devastatingly, don't bother you anymore. And so as they found that man sitting at the feet of Jesus, now the heart is right with God, and there's a calmness that comes over us. There is order in our lives. Not so confused about everything, not upset by too many things. Out of the calmness of your spirit, there is an order about you and you can go about doing that which is right and pleasing in God's sight. You are then prepared to serve, the blessing of peace will give you a calm spirit, put order in your life and make you ready to serve. You've heard me say that demon possessed man was so orderly he said at that point, can I go with you? And that's what a person will do when Jesus comes into your life. You'll want to know, "Master can I go with you?", then you will hear Him say on occasions, "no don't you go with me, go home and tell your friends about the great things the Lord has done for you."

There is a blessing of true purpose. He gives you the blessing of peace, the blessing of true purpose. Not necessarily gained, all the time. He won't just provide you pleasure in life. He won't even just merely save your soul, but He will give you God, and provide His will in your spirit, and He will make you gain the strength that your heart needs, and the unity of life - that you are able to bear your own burdens.

Thirdly, the blessing of moral advancement. The blessings that God gives. The blessing of moral advancement. Our path is onward. It's upward. The more good a man does, the nobler he becomes. Every time you do good, you wanna do some more. When you do good to others, and they see the relief, the feeling they get out of your touch, your goodness, you can't help but feel proud and happy with yourself and your accomplishments. You wanna do more good in the future. So there's a blessing of moral advancement.

By every act of self-denial and virtue man rises in dignity and strength. I want to say that again, by every act of self-denial and virtue man rises in dignity and strength. The more you give the more you got to give. See what God is into is the more you give, the more He gives to you. And as somebody wrote the song, just keep on giving. So when you have done what God has called you to do, and He's given you the dignity and strength to keep on doing it – that's moral advancement. You are moving forward not backwards.

Then there's the blessing of spiritual usefulness. Only the good can do good. You're advancing toward the kingdom when you are accepting the blessing of moral advancement and spiritual advancement. Then what the psalmist points out there is the blessing of a bright future. Life's interests are secured in your future endeavors. The outlook through all the times of cloudiness ends in light. So even though sometimes the way gets dark and it looks like you can't see out ahead of you, in front of you God is in a position to turn the light on and you can go toward the light of eternal blessings.

Finally, the blessing of God's eternal love. There is nothing worth living for other than doing good and finishing God's work. What is God's work? The work of Jesus Christ. He sent Him to show us the way, to do the right thing, to love one another as I have loved you, to keep your faith in Him who is able to deliver you from all that often besets you. God's blessing for eternal love is standing out there for you.

And so what David was pointing out in the Psalm:

"Blessed is the man that walketh not in the counsel of the ungodly. Stop listening for others to give you directions when Jesus has already given them to you, *nor sitteth in the seat of the scornful. But his delight is in the law of the Lord; and in his law doth he meditate day and night."*

The original King James Version says,

"And he shall be like a tree planted by the rivers of water, that bringeth forth his fruit in his season; his leaf also shall not wither; and whatsoever he doeth shall prosper."

Then David says, let me point out something to you

"The ungodly are not so: but are like the chaff which the wind driveth away. Therefore the ungodly shall not stand in the judgment, nor sinners in the congregation of the righteous. For the Lord knoweth the way of the righteous: but the way of the ungodly shall perish."

The blessings of God…Life's Blessings. You can think of a few can't you? The blessings that God has blessed you with. The things that He's done for you that nobody could, and even if they could, they would not. The blessings of goodness. The blessings of love and kindness. The blessings that God only can provide.

Keep your hands in God's hand and He will surely bring you out and you will always be blessed with God in your life.

Life's Blessings

God Bless You

Conquerors Through Christ

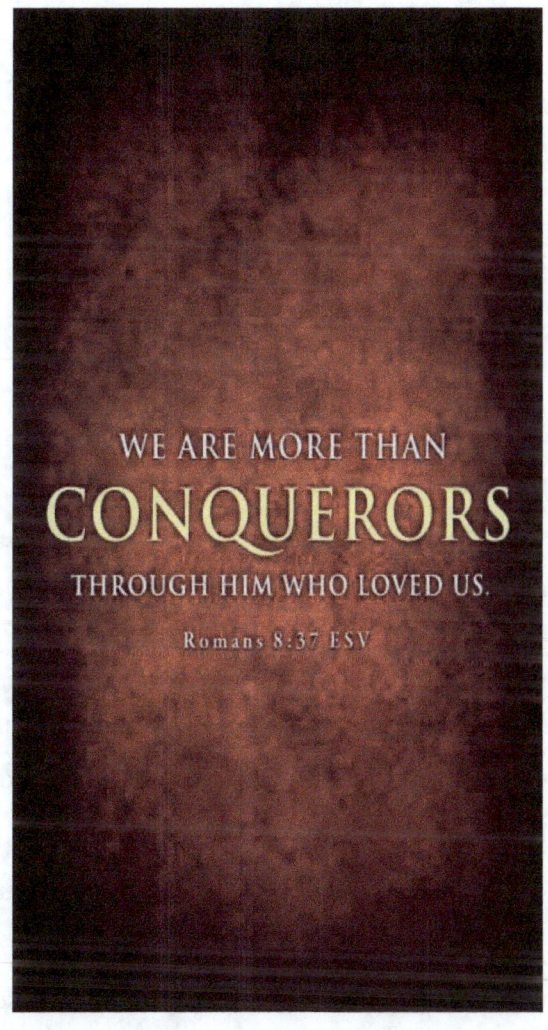

"And we know that all things work together for good to them that love God, to them who are the called according to his purpose." Romans 8:28

✝ Conquerors Through Christ

I want to share with you a sermon from the scripture found in Romans 8 verse 28, and it's a story behind that scripture that you ought to read whenever you get a chance read the entire chapter of Romans:

"And we know that all things work together for good to them that love God, to them who are called according to his purpose." (KJV)

With that scripture and your reading of the balance of that chapter, I want to talk about, "Conquerors Through Christ."

It's amazing that a person like Paul who represented a changed heart and mind that God had dealt with sometimes in the past on the Damascus road when he was what we would consider today, a Grand Rascal. He didn't believe in that Christ thing, he didn't believe in the Christian church, and he believed that that just ought to be made extinct, it should just be vanished from the Earth. And one day God stopped him as he was traveling to Damascus to destroy that church and he said he heard a voice above his head and the sunlight shone brighter as a light shined brighter than the sun, and he fell off his horse. And he heard a voice say, "Saul, Saul, why persecuteh thou me?

Is it hard to kick against the prick?" And Paul said, his name was Saul at that time, he said I asked Him, "Lord, what will you have me do?" And the Lord assigned him to go on to Damascus as you had planned, but I'm changing your name to Paul, and I'm changing your mission to help to save the church rather than trying to destroy it. And from that point Paul went forth to carry out the mission God had given him.

When you look at the scripture, and him saying, "And we know that all things work together for good to them that love God, to them who are called according to his purpose." Look at what happened to Paul after his meeting God on that Damascus road. It's remarkable that he could even make the statement, and we know that all things work together for good when he was imprisoned as a spokesman for Christ. Locked in a cage on several occasions, abused and misused. When he looked back over his life and remembered being stoned by mob crowds; he would do the preaching, they would do the stoning, but he kept preaching about Jesus.

He found himself beaten on many occasions by destructive crowds of people who gathered to do him great bodily harm, and yet when he came out, he went forth again, preaching and teaching the word of God. Paul said, I was bitten by a venomous snake. I had just come off of a shipwreck and was there on the banks of a river gathering stones for a fire to be made, and a snake bit me, and the crowd who was carrying me to prison stood there and watched when I would die from the snake bite. And they watched Paul shake the snake off, and nothing happened. He went right on preaching and teaching the Word of God.

He was shipwrecked on several occasions and almost lost his life in the waters, but God saved him. He said to the people that were with him and took him to prison: "Those of you who can swim go on to shore, those of you who cannot, pick up broken pieces of vessel and hold on till we get there, Nobody will be lost."

All things then he says work together for good for them that love the Lord. David picked it up, and this is one of the people that Paul admired in his ministry. David said something similar to what Paul was preaching that day; he said, "It's good for me that I've been afflicted that I might learn thy statutes." Here David recognized that God sometimes got to show you who He is. He's got to show you that His power is greater than yours, and there's nothing in this world you can do to out maneuver Him. So He would sometimes give David a little punishment, and David said, "it's good for me that I've been afflicted, that I may learn Thy statutes."

On another occasion David said, "before I was afflicted, I was a wayward child, and God dealt with me in the right way and brought me back to my livable style, but now he says I have kept thy word." David also pointed out, and Paul remembered that: "I was young, but now I am old. I have not seen the righteous forsaken, or God's seed begging bread."

Paul couldn't help but remember David's admission that he too, had been a grand rascal, and that God had picked him up, and propped him up, on several occasions and made him remember who he was, and who God was. And he recognized that God had been there for him ever since he was a young boy, when he took that slingshot and killed a giant of a man and stopped a war between two countries. And here he is now declaring, I was young, but now I am old, I've not seen the righteous forsaken, or God's seed begging bread.

There is a good providence that we need to look at in God. Many times we believe that the only thing good is something that we declare good – good health, good bank account, good joy, and good happiness. But we don't recognize that sometimes goodness comes through the grace of God -- where He brought us out of a situation and put us in a joyful state.

Many times we find it hard to find goodness in sickness. I know you're no different from me as far as sickness is concerned- you don't want to be sick. But sometimes the only way you can find a relationship with God is through sickness. You remember the story of the woman who had the issue of blood for twelve years. She had spent her bank account. She had done everything possible to find a cure, and she couldn't find one. And in her sickness with all of the trials and troubles she had been through, one day she heard about Jesus. And she heard that Jesus had the power to heal sickness. And she said, I've got to go find that man, I've got to see Him. And she went down in a crowd of people following Jesus and pressing and pushing trying to get closer, and closer to him. And somebody wanted to know from her "Woman, why are you pushing everybody away trying to get to this man." And she said, Let me tell you something. I believe enough in this man to know that if I could just touch the hem of His garment – 'I'll be made whole."

As she was falling she touched Him, and Jesus stopped and said, somebody touched me. His disciples looked at Him and said, Master, you got to be out of your mind with all these people pushing and shoving trying to get next to you, and you say, somebody touched you. He said, naw, this is different. I felt the spirit going out of me. Somebody touched me. And when He looked upon that woman he said, "thou faith has made you whole."

Don't you know that sometimes you are going to have adversity? You just don't like hard times, trials, and tribulations. But sometimes the only way you can find God is through your adversity. Job one day got caught up in a situation where God and satan was having a conversation. God asked Satan, "where you been?" And "where you going?" He said, "I'm coming from walking up and down in the world, going to and fro trying to see what I could devour." God said to him, "have you considered my servant Job?" He said, "yes, I considered him. I know Job, I know his reputation in the community. I know he serves you, and he prays all the time. But I do know this, if you let me have him. If you would take the hedge from around him, I'll make him curse you to your face". And God said to him, "no, I know Job better than that, I'm going to let you touch him, I'll let you bother him, but you leave his life to me." Satan got after Job and took everything he had. Destroyed his wealth, his health, his family. Somebody said to him, "Job, why don't you just go ahead and curse God, and die." Job said, "No, of all my appointed times, will I wait till my change comes." He said, "this stuff I had, the Lord giveth, the Lord taketh away, blessed be the name of the Lord. And of all of my appointed times, I'm just gone wait here till me change come." It was in his adversity that he discovered that God's Will was greater at the end, than it was at the beginning.

Look at poverty. Many of us go through these poverty stricken times. We don't have much of anything. Sometimes we can't get the next meal in the house. Look at the number of people who have lost their jobs, and lost their health, and lost their wealth, everything in the last six months and yet people can't understand why they keep trusting God. People in this Christian race look at the man who went up to the temple one day to ask for alms, to beg for something for bread for a way to pay the rent. And he discovered Peter and John going to church, and the man was there at the steps of the church begging. And he asked Peter and John for some pennies to buy some bread, and Peter said, "I know your poverty. I know what you're here for, but today I want you to look on us." The man raised his head. Peter said, "silver and gold have I none, but such as I have, give I thee. In the name of Jesus Christ of Nazareth, rise up and walk." And that beggar, in his poverty, stood up with strengthened legs and feet, and said he went hopping and then jumping, and running, and praising God. Makes no difference about your situation, God is in a position to heal you!

There are those in sorrow who have felt that they could not lift the load, and dump the load of burdens on their shoulders, and yet they kept their faith in God. Somebody said to them quietly, don't worry about it. Weeping may endure for a night, but joy comes in the morning.

And so sometimes we have to go through sickness, and adversity, poverty, sorrow to know what God can do, and what He will do. Paul then believed that human nature in itself is unholy. We're alienated from Him, easily influenced by the present world, and easily led by temptation and sin. He further believes that if God only allows sunshine, no rain, fair weather and no storms, good health and no pain, we would not see the need for repentance.

So, He finally winds his communications up with, "all things work together for good." He says, we know that all things work together for good to them that love God, to them who are called according to His purpose. And those of us who have had experience with that like to sing occasionally; the road is rough, the going gets tough, and the hills are hard to climb. But I started out a long time ago, and I'm determined to keep Jesus in mind. I'm tired and weary, but I must travel on till the Lord comes and calls me away. Finally, one says, I'm going where the wicked shall cease from troubling, the weary shall be at rest, and all of the saints of the ages can sit at His feet and be blessed.

What will I do? Jesus says, " I'll be with you" So we all know, as Paul went on to finish up that Chapter 8 as you read it, he says, *"so who shall separate us from the love of Christ? Shall tribulation, or distress, or persecution, or famine, or nakedness, or peril, or sword."* As it is written for their sake we are killed all the day long. We are counted as sheep for the slaughter. He says, nay, naw, in all these things we are more than conquerors through Him that loved us. *"For I am persuaded that neither death, nor life, nor angels, nor principalities, nor powers, nor things present, nor things to come, nor height, nor depth, nor any other creature shall be able to separate us from the love of God, which is in Christ Jesus, our Lord."*

So, yes, we can be more than conquerors through Jesus Christ, our Lord.

God Bless You

Man's Lack of Knowledge of Himself

"And he said, I tell thee, Peter, the cock shall not crow this day, before that thou shalt thrice deny that thou knowest me." Luke 21:34

✝ Man's Lack of Knowledge of Himself

"And he said, I tell thee, Peter, the cock shall not crow this day, before that thou shalt thrice deny that thou knowest me." Luke 21:34

As I begin my message today, I want to make an announcement before going into the message, and this is particularly of interest to all of the people listening online, and who are enjoying the services from home and other places. We're going to officially return to worship in the church on next Sunday, and I'm still asking for your consideration in handling the pandemic in a safe way. We will still respect the distancing in the church, the Sanctuary. We'll also respect wearing the mask. Even though I don't have mine on right now when I'm speaking, but I do have it in my pocket, and I will have it on as soon as I finish. And so we're inviting you to not only trust your faith, but trust your ability to do what is right according to the norms of our society. And so we expect you. We have just the one service, and that's at 8:30 on Sunday morning, and it will only be an hour long so be here on time.

Let me share with you now a scripture from the gospel of Luke, the twenty-second chapter, and I want to read verses thirty one through thirty four in your hearing:

"And the Lord said, Simon, Simon, behold, Satan hath desired to have you, that he may sift you as wheat: But I have prayed for thee, that thy faith fail not: and when thou art converted, strengthen thy brethren. And he said unto him, Lord, I am ready to go with thee, both into prison, and to death. And he said, I tell thee, Peter, the cock shall not crow this day, before that thou shalt thrice deny that thou knowest me." (KJV)

I want to talk for a little while from this topic: "Man's Lack of Knowledge of Himself." Now remember again what Peter said to Jesus when he told him that Satan had desired him. He said, Lord, I am ready to go with thee, both into prison, and to death. And Jesus answered him back, in a word Peter, before the cock crows, you will deny me not twice, but thrice- three times. And so let me just share with you my thoughts on Man's Lack of Knowledge of Himself.

In some ways Peter represents all of us. He believes himself capable of withstanding any dare, enduring any extremity in the cause of Christ. Look at how he mistook himself. We ought to know ourselves well, but we don't. We suppose ourselves to be strong and steadfast, when in fact were feeble and unreliable. We suppose ourselves to be humble minded, but in fact, in reality we are proud of heart. We suppose ourselves to be generous, but when you get down to it we are really self-serving and self-seeking. We suppose ourselves to be devout, but most of the time we are unspiritual. We believe many times that we are close to God or very near Him, when we are, in fact, far off. And so, whatever we think of ourselves and our relationship with God may satisfy us for the moment but it is not a true and satisfactorily, reliable answer of our relationship with God.

Look at God's knowledge of us, and I think you will find God's knowledge of us is different from our knowledge of ourselves. You see, God knows our heart. God knows how sincere our purpose in life; whether we are simply putting on, pretending. God knows deep down in our hearts the reality of ourselves, of the things we trust in and believe in. And so we recognize that our belief falls short of who we are. But, God is looking straight into the inner sanctum of our hearts. It has already been declared scripturally that out of the heart comes the issues of life, and as a man thinketh in his heart, so is he. And so He knows the sincerity of our purpose.

God knows how frequent our efforts are. Sometimes we convince ourselves that we've done so much, and we're so tired of doing what we do for the Lord until we just gone rest – we not gone do nothing else. But God knows the amount of time we spend, the effort we give in the services of His kingdom, and He can tell us right now whether we measure up or falter by the way. He knows our efforts.

God knows how many of our disappointments fail us in life. He knows how faulty our nature is. God knows how wounded and weak our spirits are. He knows whether we can stand up under the pressure of life, the troubles and trials we must endure-God knows whether or not we have the stamina, the stick-to-itiveness to hang in there until He blesses us with the blessings He sees fit.

God knows our life. He knows the way we take. We may decide what will be our journey, where we will head in life, how we will get there, and how we will end up if we do it this way or that way, but if we fail to ask God to guide us, to protect us, to give us the courage to stand in the face of danger, and all the things that so of beset us, we're going to be failures along the way. But since we know that God knows the way we take, we should ask Him, "Lord be with me, guide me every step of the way."

God knows the path we are about to pursue. I don't care how young and how old we are at this moment in time, God already knows the path we either have taken, or plan to take. And if you are young and about to start life, to do it with all of the greatness you can endure, and muster- then you ought to tell God, Lord be with me while I run this race, cause I don't want to run this race in vain.

See, God knew more about Peter than he knew of himself. Peter was a good friend of Jesus, he showed himself a real honorable person in following Jesus. Peter was the man leading the fisherman at the sea doing his business every day on the ships, and Jesus went out when He was calling His disciples, and saw Peter and his crew working hard as fishermen. And Jesus hollered out there on the boat, Hey, follow me, and I'll make you fishers of men. When Jesus made that command, He already knew the dedication of Peter and his crew. Here were men who could fish all night and catch nothing, and go back the next night, and fish again. They felt that some days you win, and some days you lose, but you've got to keep on fighting the good fight.

So when Jesus said to them, Follow me, and I'll make you fishers of men, they dropped their net, walked off that water, to follow Jesus to an unknown destination. They had no way of getting information in advance, what the success or failure of this following Jesus would amount to. But, I guess Peter was sharp enough to know that if he could spend some days and some nights fishing and catching nothing that it wouldn't be no worse following Jesus to fish for men. So he dropped his net, and followed Jesus.

He became a good friend of Jesus, a personal friend. He was one of three that were in the inner sanctum of Jesus; Peter, James, and John became personal friends of Jesus. And here on this particular day, Peter is declaring his loyalty to his master. His master is saying to them, I'm going away. That's what I came for. I came that you may have life and have it more abundantly. I'm not staying here! So I'm going. Here He was giving His farewell message to em, and Peter said, Lord, let just share this with you. I'm ready to go where you go. If you go to prison, I'm going with you. If you go to death, I'll die with you. At one point Peter showed Him, see I've got my sword. And one day he got a little frustrated there, a man had got him all heated up and Peter cut his ear off. Jesus reached down and picked the ear up, and put it back on the man's head, and said, "Peter he that lives by the sword, shall die by the sword."

But Peter wanted to be sure he showed Jesus that he was all man. And if he needed a fight, he was prepared to fight. One this particular occasion, Jesus knew the heart of Peter. He knew he loved Him. He knew he was a hard worker. He knew he was dedicated. He knew he was a righteous man; he had been with Him since that call from the sea shore to follow me and I'll make you fishers of men. Peter had been there. And now Peter is trying to convince Him, Lord, you don't have to worry about your safety. I'm here for you, and if you can't manage it, we'll go down together. Jesus said to him, Peter, let me share with you something you don't know about yourself. He said tonight before the cock crows early at daybreak, you will have already denied me three times.

And sure enough, people were standing in the yard watching them take Jesus to the courtrooms and then to Calvary. Couple of women said to the crowd, "that man there is one of them." And he said, "No, you don't know who you're talking about, I'm not the man." One of the men said, "Yea, I know him- he was in the crowd-he's one of cm." And Peter denied it again. And as Jesus was being taken to the courts, chained, He just passed Peter walking up that road, and the cock crew, and Jesus looked at Peter, and Peter cried.

Jesus knew more about him than he knew about himself. And all the promises he could make, the guarantees he gave- Lord, I'm there with you every step of the way, don't you worry about it. Jesus knew his heart. He knew he loved him. But He knew he was a weak creature.

Sometimes you make promises you can't keep. Sometimes you promise people that you can do great things, and you know you can't do it. So, he kept going. Jesus knew that Peter was a good man. He knew that he was a loving spirit. Jesus knew that Peter loved him. But sometimes he just thought he could do more than he could. But Jesus knew he was a man that could be left to carry out the mission of the kingdom.

Jesus knew that he was a trusted friend. Even though sometimes he got in a rage, and wanted to do battle. But Jesus knew that Peter was a trusted friend. Sometimes we don't know our limits. How far we can go, or how far we are able to go. But thank God Jesus knows. He knows me. He knows you. He knows just how much we can bear. And so in the crisis of the moment every day of our life, struggling against the tide, it's a good thing to know that Jesus knows, and that He'll be with us in our going out, and in our coming in.

So you keep trusting Him. Don't put too much trust in yourself. Stop bragging about what you did and what you gone do. Do like old folks used to do – tell them, "if the Lord be with me, I'll do it." So yes, man wrestles many times with what he can do, and what he knows about himself. But he missed the point often, failed many times. But thank God we know one that knows us. He will guide us around the pitfalls of life. He will protect us in our going out, and our coming in. He will lift us when we fall, and He will prop us on every leaning side. This Jesus I'm talking about, knows all about us.

God Bless You

The Obligation to Persevere

"Oh that my head were waters, and mine eyes a fountain of tears, that I might weep day and night for the slain of the daughter of my people! Oh that I had in the wilderness a lodging place of wayfaring men; that I might leave my people, and go from them! For they be all adulterers, an assembly of treacherous men." Jeremiah 9:1-2

✝ The Obligation to Persevere

For the message today, let me take you to the book of Jeremiah, the ninth chapter, and I want to read just two verses beginning with verse one, verses one and two:

Oh that my head were waters, and mine eyes a fountain of tears, that I might weep day and night for the slain of the daughter of my people! Oh that I had in the wilderness a lodging place of wayfaring men; that I might leave my people, and go from them! For they be all adulterers, an assembly of treacherous men. (KJV)

I want to take the message from those two verses and talk about "The Obligation to Persevere." I've always admired Jeremiah. He was a very human prophet, he did what he thought was necessary under any and all conditions, but he never tried to hide his own personal self.

He's called the weeping prophet. He would cry in a minute. Jeremiah wanted the world to know that if he had a place in the wilderness where wayfaring men gathered, he would go and be amongst them and hide himself from the problems of the day.

Jeremiah was an unusual human prophet. He takes us into the secret chamber of his life, his misgivings and questionings. Jeremiah was a prophet in some of the saddest days of Jerusalem… we can relate to that. We can understand sadness and sorrow. We can understand how a city, state or nation can go from the glory of the moment to the tragedy of the times, and you can't do anything but weep over it. Jeremiah wished he could just escape, and I'm sure we've had that feeling ourselves if I could just leave it all to escape for a moment to recollect myself and get myself back on track. Jeremiah said in his wishing he could escape, *"Oh that I had in the wilderness a lodging place of wayfaring men that I might leave my people and go from them."* (Jeremiah 9:2) He was a praying man. Even though his classification was a prophet, you don't necessarily have to be a prophet to pray, but Jeremiah was a praying man in all situations. He prayed to be set free on an occasion to just enjoy himself; that's awful isn't it? "Lord if I can just be free enough to enjoy myself for a day and not worry about the things that I'm worrying about. I want to be without responsibility." Jeremiah had stood the test of time, he had preached to the wayfaring, he had tried to save the lost. He did everything he thought was possible to save a dying world, but on this occasion, he just prayed to be set free so that could enjoy himself for just a moment. You know what that means, set free from your responsibilities? Have you realized that most of the things we do every day have nothing to do with self? It has to do with our responsibility to others, and what we can do to save a dying world. He prayed that he could just go where all men go, and be where you can relax on the beach in your own thoughts. When you look at the fact that we have been shut down… the things we truly enjoy doing, we can't enjoy right now. Sometimes it would feel good to just go and lie on the beach and roll the sand through your toes, and feel good about being away from the responsibilities that you carry every day.

Jeremiah prayed that he would just go where no one knows you, and you can do what you want to. Now and then you have those moments where friends can't cut it, family won't do, you just want to and need to be by yourself in nature… by the running waters, and on the sand beach of time. Jeremiah said I want to go and just watch the streets from the balcony. I just want to get up out of the crowd, watch what's going on, and I don't want anybody to bother me. I just want to be able to look down on the crowd as they go and enjoy themselves. He prayed that's where he can do acts of kindness with friendliness.

Look at the temptation to escape, as I mentioned, just being free from responsibility. What do you call your responsibility? The heavy load that you're carrying. That responsibility of having to do what is right and pleasing in God's sight, and being able to do what family needs. Responsibility that you didn't create for yourself, but is heaped upon you, heavy loads. You may just want to escape from busy schedules. Have you ever noticed that no matter how many things you plan for your life each day, you don't ever catch up? You can't ever finish all of the schedule that you made for yourself, and the schedule that others have laid on you? You work from can to can't, from early to late, and you go to bed at night unfinished in order to get up the next morning with the same schedule.

The temptation to escape includes even business increases. You know people who go into business for themselves, wish for success, work at success, pray for success, but there are times when even the business keeps on getting on your nerves! You just need a place that you can escape to for a little respite…to go and try it all over again. While you are busy with your heavy loads, and busy schedules, and increase in business, the community's influence is there. You gotta keep on working for others at the same time and doing all you can for the people around you.

You've got to have and keep your home responsibilities all while you are doing all of these other things! A few days ago, I cut all the grass around my house, and it was looking so pretty when I finished; and three days later, all that grass was back around my house, and I got to cut it all over again; so it's a responsibility that keeps coming back, and you can't do anything but just do what you can and cry out for a little rest time.

Public responsibilities: Oh, we are running all over the land right now just trying to figure out how we survive this pandemic. How do we get past this treacherous virus? This thing that nobody seems to be able to understand yet, and how will we fix it when we understand it. But it's a public responsibility that we all must work on at the same time while carrying all of these other heavy loads.

Jeremiah prayed he would just like to get away from these thankless days. You do all you can do, all you're able to, and you got a thankless world that you're working for and they don't even care whether you succeed or fail. Jeremiah said I want to be free from the monotony of day after day. Everything goes over and over and over again. Some of you had the privilege of hearing me say one time in a sermon before that one of the things that happens in marriages is that you thought you fell in love, and you were just going to be in love for the rest of your life, and you have a good time loving. The woman found herself having to get up every day at the same time to make breakfast, then lunch, then dinner, and you better have some snacks in between. You then have to do the same cleanup, in the same house, in the same rooms, day after day after day and you never get caught up because something else interferes and you have to come back later and try to finish what you started earlier. There was a time when the men were called upon to go to work and then there were what we called "housewives." That doesn't happen any more because she's got to go to work too. Every day of your life is over and over and over again. It becomes a monotonous life where you don't ever catch up, you don't ever finish, you can't ever quit.

The Obligation to Persevere

Jeremiah said I'm just tired of the monotony of day after day and he said it doesn't just happen day after day. These days go into weeks, and the weeks go into months, and the months go into spring, winter, summer, and fall. Nothing changes, just you're tired of the monotony of it all!

We need to free ourselves! Jeremiah says we want to think we can escape, but we carry our hearts with us and whenever you go, and wherever you go, and whatever you try to do, you carry the same burden to where you just went. The one thing you can't get away from is you. If you catch a plane to go to the other side of the world, you have put "you" on that plane. When you land on the other side of the world, you have landed you at that spot. You're carrying your burdens, you're carrying the schedules, you're carrying the increase, you're carrying the influences, you're carrying the responsibilities, you're carrying all the lost and last days.

But we carry our hearts with us and in our hearts, we have the weakness that often besets us. We have the limitations that we've had all the time. Jeremiah says if I could just go to a place where the wayfaring people live, just turn all this stuff loose, and come back after I get a little rest. But there is the obligation to persevere. God has sent him to be separate from other men. God calls us out to do a job, to do a task and when He calls us out to do it, He's got all of his people in mind and He gives you your responsibility to help save His people from whatever it is that's troubling them. He has sent us to be separate from other people. He didn't call us to watch from the balcony. Oh, it would be nice, wouldn't it? It would be so nice to just watch the goings on down in the streets and you can sit in a high spot and just look down on wayfaring men. But God didn't call us to just watch from the balcony. He has called us to get on the streets and watch from there to do what we can for a suffering humanity, for a dying world. He wants us to be down on the ground, to be our own housekeepers, to grow familiar with our surroundings.

So we don't have the luxury of just watching from some distant place. God has called us as He's called Jeremiah to get down on the ground and become familiar with the suffering of His people. He needs to be down there so He can see habits grow, and falsehoods betray itself. Heneeds to be there so He can see sons and daughter wrestle with the sins of their parent. Oh, if I could just go out in the wilderness, and live amongst wayfaring men; that I might leave my people and go from them.

But no, I have an obligation to persevere. I've got to keep going. I've got to keep walking in the path of right and righteousness. I've got to keep crying out, "give me your hand, silver and gold have I none but such as I have, give I thee."

Church, you have an obligation to persevere. You've got to keep on traveling the King's highway and yes, you will get tired, you will suffer loss, you will feel the need for somebody to care; but even when you have to walk alone, you must continue to persevere!

God Bless You

Equal Sacrifices

"But this I say, He which soweth sparingly shall reap also sparingly; and he which soweth bountifully shall reap also bountifully. Every man according as he purposeth in his heart, so let him give; not grudgingly, or of necessity: for God loveth a cheerful giver."
2 Corinthians 9:6-7

† Equal Sacrifices

Let me share with you a scripture from **2 Corinthians 9:6-7:**

"But this I say, He which soweth sparingly shall reap also sparingly; and he which soweth bountifully shall reap also bountifully. Every man according as he purposeth in his heart, so let him give; not grudgingly, or of necessity: for God loveth a cheerful giver." (KJV)

I want to do a dual teaching and preaching message today, because I'm going to say to those of you who are family and friends of this broadcast that every so often all of us need to come together, and do what is right for the common good. In order to produce and project services from this church on Sundays, and we've been doing it since the pandemic launched upon us, there are times when we need some support to keep the work of Christ going. Therefore, I'm going to say to you as you listen to me today that I want to tell you what the scripture says about equal sacrifices. That's the topic of my message today- "Equal Sacrifice."

You know when you look at scripture both in the Old and New Testaments, it is filled with the responsibility of the Christian worker, the person who follows the teachings of God, the teachings of Jesus Christ, and how important it is to give to Him that which is due for His work and His services. There is no better indicator of growth in the Christian life than in the area of giving.

Many times, we look at giving as only dollars and cents. That's not always the case. But we have come to a point where we have allowed dollars and cents to be the driving force of all that we do in all of our accomplishments. On the dollar bill it states *"in God we trust,"* and in another place on that dollar bill it tells us or says to us *"e pluribus Unum."* Some of us have come to believe that the only way to give and the only way to survive in this world is to match it by the worth of the dollar. There are times when you do need the dollar, but not in every case when you are giving of yourself. In this case, I'm saying to you, as you praise and worship with us each Sunday, we do need a dollar.

In the book of Deuteronomy 16:17 it says:

"Every man shall give as he is able, according to the blessing of the Lord thy God which he hath given thee." (KJV)

So God is not calling upon us to make any real sacrifices. He's just calling upon us to return to Him that portion of what He has given us to keep his work going. So God gives. First, He gave us life, He gives us health and strength, and He gives us the ability to go forth and earn for ourselves a living, and to do what is good and pleasing in His sight. He only gives or expects us to give back to Him the portion of that portion that we received from Him.

Proverbs 23:26 says:

"My son, give me thine heart, and let thine eyes observe my ways." (KJV)

Christians, God says, give me your heart, and take your eyes and watch what I do. You will be able to see the results of my blessings that I placed upon you. You may not be able to explain them to a great degree of satisfaction, but if you give me your heart, then you watch with your eyes what I do. Jesus came forth repeating that same message, and we have to be sure that as we build our Christian life, and a Christian worth that we are looking upon the blessings of God from day to day, to give us what we need to make it right for the world we live in, and the people we serve.

Look at what Luke 6:38 says in the New Testament.

"Give, and it shall be given unto you; good measure, pressed down, and shaken together, and running over, shall men give into your bosom. For with the same measure that ye mete withal it shall be measured to you again." (KJV)

Some of you know for a historical fact that I'm an old country boy. I was born and raised in the cotton fields of Alabama, and I had to work each day of my life to glean from the earth the food we ate. Everything we got, we had to grow it, till it, and harvest it from the fields to survive in the world. We lived in a community of kin folks, and some strangers who had come into the community. Houses were placed apart; they were not built like the urban areas. There was land between them and sometimes you had to walk a mile to get to the next house. But I used to try and figure out why when a mother sent a child to our house to ask my mother for some meal, and they brought their own bucket with them. It was absolutely necessary for mama to give the orders, "take this bucket and fill it with meal." It was in a big drum, and we had ground the meal, and put it in for food for the future, and she would say "take this bucket and fill it with meal." Then she would order, "shake it so the meal packs down, and the bucket is really full." You don't just come get a few cups of meal dumped off in the bucket, and somebody's asking you for some meal to cook some bread. But that house would say, "shake it down," and that bucket would be shaken until the meal ran over. Then as I read the scriptures, they weren't doing anything but what Jesus said do, *"good measure pressed down, and shaken together and running over shall man give unto your bosom for with the same measure that ye meet withal it shall be measured to you again."* (Luke 6:38)

So you ought to keep in mind that when you're doing your duty, and giving out blessings and grace, you ought to give, so when you get it back, you get a full measure of somebody's love and compassion. So even though we lived in a situation where we didn't have much, we had to grow our own corn, take it to the gristmill, have it ground up, bring it back to the house, and put it in the barrel. It was enough meal in that barrel of not only this house, but anybody else's house that needed some meal for bread that day. And nobody was trying to cheat anybody, shake it down, fill it up. And that's how we survived in this world with little of nothing, because each one of us who had something shared it with somebody else. Jesus taught that way back in the New Testament in Luke, when He said blessings should be shaken down.

And so in the book of Acts, Peter watched a man one day coming to the temple, he and John were going to worship and they had seen a man come daily to the door of the temple, to beg alms, to beg some change, to beg something from people who had it to give as they went into the church to worship. On this particular day, Peter had had enough of this same man coming to beg for alms. He's got to pay his rent, he's got to pay for food, has got to buy whatever he can, but doesn't have a job, doesn't even have the health and strength to go and do it! So he came and sat at the foot of the steps and begged each day. Peter and John had had enough. When that man came that day, Peter stood up to him and said, *"Silver and gold have I none, but such as I have give I thee. In the name of Jesus Christ of Nazareth rise up and walk."* (Acts 3:6-16)

Now, you can ask for all the pennies you want, and somebody can give you some change every time they see you, but that is not satisfying the need you have. He needed health and strength, he needed the ability to walk, he needed the ability to go and get a job, and buy his own food; so Peter said, "Give me your hand. I want you to know that silver and gold have I none... I'm broke too! *"Silver and gold have I none. But such as I have, give I thee." ((KJV), Acts 3:6)* Now here's what Peter had as *the "such that I have"*; *In the name of Jesus Christ of Nazareth, rise up and walk."* You may not have what somebody is asking for, but I know you have what they need. If you got Jesus, that's enough! You can help a person get up on their feet and go on about their business.

And then that scripture that I brought as the scripture for the text

2 Corinthians 9:7 says:

"Every man according as he purposeth in his heart, so let him give; not grudgingly, or of necessity: for God loveth a cheerful giver." (KJV)

In other words, it ought to be in your heart to give, not have to be asked all the time to keep God's worship alive. Three things I want to say briefly about the attitude of giving. First of all, I want to ask, what is your attitude? The Bible is calling us to do what is good and what is right on behalf of others, to do what God has blessed us with, and give back portions of what He has given us. So I ask what is your attitude? Are you willing? Tell me if you are cheerful while you are giving, or is that something you're just doing to match what somebody else is doing? It ought to come from your heart. Not sparingly, not grudgingly, for God loves a cheerful giver.

The second thing I want to say about that is, what is your motive? Did you give as your Christian duty and responsibility because the pastor asked you to? Do you tell me that your religion is so weak that somebody has to remind you to give? And then you want to call the preacher a begging preacher! Or did you give because the competition was watching? You know what the competition is? The neighbor down the street that sees you driving that new car, enjoying yourself every day, and then you go to church and they happen to be at the church with you. And now when the offering comes around, are you giving just because you want your neighbor to see you giving? Are you just competing with the competition? Or did it come from the heart? Or, are you guilty of something that you want God to look over? Done so many things wrong, and out of place that you are just begging for a blessing, and you just need God to see you. "God, see I'm here and you see my offering" that's not the reason we ought to be giving.

We say "well I gave because God requires it." God didn't require it. He told you to make up your mind, and He gave you a formula so that you would know what was right in His sight. See, God prepared a way for everybody, poor, rich or whatever, to give the same amount to His Christian work. He said I'm going to require the tithe from you. I'm going to require a penny out of a dime, a dime out of a dollar, a dollar out of ten dollars, ten dollars out of a hundred, and one hundred dollars out of a thousand. Now can you imagine having that kind of leeway that the God who gave you all of this is only requiring that? If you have the motive to make it because you feel good, it ought to be because you love the Lord. I love the Lord. Somebody wrote, *"I love the Lord, He heard my cry and pitied every groan Long as I live, and trouble rise I'll hasten to His throne."*

Finally, the third thing I want to ask you, what is the formula? I asked you what your attitude is. Now, what is your motive? Now what is the formula? The formula simply is, it must be regular. How can you expect to live out of the meal you bought yesterday- it's gone! You need another one for today, don't you? Have you noticed that we have three meals that even the doctors and medical people tell you are important to you; breakfast, lunch, and dinner. Then some people go so far as to say that your most important meal is breakfast…get your body started. Then, after dinner, the Lord will lay you down to sleep. The body requires eight hours of sleep to get you fine-tuned for breakfast tomorrow. But every day you have to go through the same ritual every day. That's the way God made us and we can't do anything but follow his construct. That is the formula that we must live on, and we must do for God's work every day. He broke it down so easily. He gave us on the first day of the week, being systematic, He says let everyone of you lay by Him in store. (1 Corinthians 16:2) Now, if God has required of you a small portion of what He has given you, you ought to lay it up in store. Stop going by the dresser saying, "Oh, I think I'll use the church money", or "I'm broke today, I ain't going to pay nothing to the Christian cause." He says lay it up in store. So He's made you a trustee of His wealth, His money, and told you on the first day of the week, bring it, give it to my house.

Finally, be proportionate. As equal as God has prepared you and prospered you, it's equal. I just pointed out a penny, a dime, a dollar… I pointed all that out. That means you can't give no more than anybody else. It's all equal.

And so today, as I conclude this message, I'm asking everyone under the sound of my voice to give something to the work of Christ at this church. In order for us to continue, I'm asking everybody who listens to me today to send a donation. It's your time to do what you can, and you will help the cause.

God Bless you, and God Keep you

A Good Mother

"And thou shalt teach them diligently unto thy children, and shalt talk of them when thou sittest in thine house, and when thou walkest by the way, and when thou liest down, and when thou risest up."
Deuteronomy 6:8

A Good Mother

Since today is a day of celebration honoring mothers in our society, in our world, I want to take this time and present a message to mothers everywhere, and I titled this sermon, "A Good Mother". In the book of Deuteronomy, in the Old Testament one of the five books of law, chapter 6, verses five through nine. Maybe I ought to back it up to verse four through nine. Let me read it:

"Hear, O Israel: The Lord our God is one Lord:
And thou shalt love the Lord thy God with all thine heart, and with all thy soul, and with all thy might. And these words, which I command thee this day, shall be in thine heart: And thou shalt teach them diligently unto thy children, and shalt talk of them when thou sittest in thine house, and when thou walkest by the way, and when thou liest down, and when thou risest up. And thou shalt bind them for a sign upon thine hand, and they shall be as frontlets between thine eyes.

And thou shalt write them upon the posts of thy house, and on thy gates." (KJV)

Let me bring up a point first that I would like you to remember. Your success as a family, our success as a society depends not on what happens at the White House, but what happens inside your house. There is no way to be a perfect mother, but there are a million ways to be a good mother. Let me repeat that again; there is no way to be a perfect mother, but a million ways to be a good mother.

Now look at Deuteronomy chapter 6 again verses six through nine: And thou shalt love the Lord thy God with all thine heart, and with all thy soul, and with all thy might. And these words, which I command thee this day, shall be in thine heart: Not on a piece of paper somewhere, or on a table in a dusty Bible, but somewhere. You can print it and paste it to the refrigerator. But these words, the words of God, and the words of love shall be in your heart:

"And thou shalt teach them diligently unto thy children, and shalt talk of them when thou sittest in thine house."

There ought to be some conversation around the house that there is more than just the normal day to day- what you did? - What you doing? What you didn't do? Where you been? What Moses points out in the law book of Deuteronomy when he came back from talking with God, is that when you sit down in your house as a mother you ought to call to remembrance the things that God has done for you, the things that God can do, and will do! And teach your children how to love God as you do. You should do this when you're walking down the road- just having a walk and talk to your children about the blessings of the Lord. You ought to do it so faithfully, that even when you lie down you ought to be talking about the goodness of God, what He's done, what He will do.

When you rise up in the morning, you ought to let your children see you thank God for watching over me all night long, and then touching me with a finger of love, letting me rise up early this morning. You ought to spread love everywhere you go. Some people recognize that you can't always be with your mother all of the time, but it's a beautiful thing if you find a surrogate, a substitute somewhere along the way that's teaching the same thing, and living the same life, and praising the same God. Let no one ever come to you without leaving happier. So, it's not just about your house. It's about your mother's house- down the street, up the street, across the road, everybody ought to see, and sense there is a mother in the place.

Let me share with you some things that you ought to remember as I remember. I want to share with you a few mothers' sayings.

"What part of no you don't understand?" Remember that?

Or as you fight with your siblings or somebody close to you, your mama says, "What's going on?" And you say, she started it! And your mama says, "I don't care who started it, I want it cut out!"

Haven't you ever said, 'mama she won't give me none of what she's got?' And your mama says, "Your hands are not broken." And then you cry out, that is so unfair! Your mother says, "Life is not fair."

And she comes home in the evening and finds you jumping on the bed, and she says to you, "the bed is not made to jump on, you best go to sleep."

And then one day you aggravate her to the point when she says, "you're just getting on my nerves. I'm telling your daddy when he gets home."

Then you cry out while having a good dinner one day, you want a little bit more of what you've been enjoying, and you see the last piece of meat about to be taken, you reach at it, and somebody else reaches at it, your mama says, "eat your vegetables."

And then one day she asks you a question that requires an answer immediately, and you can't come up with an answer, and you just say, "I don't know." And your mother says, "I don't know is not an answer."

Or when you said, "why do I have to do that? Mama says, "because I said so, that's why!"

When you look at love, the rules of love, you find sometimes you not only have pure love and sweet love. Sometimes you have to get love that got a little toughness to it. It has to come back at you, and make you do the right thing, the right way.

I remember, and this I'm saying to all of the mothers who've lost their mother, and people who have lost someone that is close and dear to them. On April 3, 2002, I lost my mother, and that was the same woman that gave me birth on April 3rd, and decided she would leave me and go home on April 3rd. I've pinned this letter that I think is appropriate. It speaks to a lot of hearts when it comes to mothers. It's a letter to a mother gone, written on the day God took her home:

"A million times I've needed you, a million times I've cried. If love alone could have saved you, you never would have died. In life I loved you dearly, in death I'll love you still. In my heart you hold a place that no one could ever fill. It broke my heart to lose you, but you didn't go alone. A part of me went with you the day God took you home."

Keep in mind mothers that your success as a family, our success as a society, depends not on what goes on at the White House, but what goes on inside your house. God has called upon mothers in a very special way to be a loving and caring person. And I can assure you God had in mind the family construct when He made man from the dust of the Earth. When He had the whole universe He decided that man should not live alone, so He took him, took a rib, and made a woman, and called her a woman, and she became the first fruit to all that is.

She bore sons, raised children, dug in the fields, brought food in the house and kept on working toward a higher order for the family. And God sent one more message down by Moses, Tell her that, *"Thou shalt love the Lord thy God with all thine heart, with all thy soul, with all thy might."* *"And thou shalt teach them diligently unto thy children and shall talk of Him when thou sitteth in thy house, and when thy walketh by the way, and when thy liest down, and when thou sitteth up. And thy shalt bind them for a sign upon thine hand, and they shall be as frontlets between thine eyes. And thou shalt write them upon the posts of thine house. Write them at your gate."* (Deuteronomy 6:7-9)

Women, you have been called upon by God to do a wonderful job, and you cannot ever expect to be a perfect person – you can't be a perfect person. But you can be a good woman, and for some, a good mother.

God Bless You

 Acknowledgements

Thanks to my mother, the cause of it all, and the memory of my father, whose memory of my father, whose life is so deeply embedded in my heart.

And to my five children: David, Rosemary, Bonita, RaShon and LaDawn, who serve as a back-up to undiscovered knowledge.

The preparation of a book of sermons requires many hours of transcribing from recordings, from the pulpit, and printed materials; typing, re-typing and more re-typing. Bonita, my second daughter, spent many hours of her own time in the evenings and weekends typing this book. For this I am grateful.

Thanks Allison McClung for recording every word uttered.

This work could not have been possible without the full cooperation and assistance of Gerald Williams operating the sound room and producing the messages on social media.

Acknowledgements

A special word of thanks to Keisha Graves, the Pastor's Assistant, for keeping my office intact and shielding me from problems that could be held or solved by others.

Last, but far from the least, thanks to my wife Mary Jean, who encouraged me to put my thoughts in writing.

I am grateful to Dr. Filbert Martin for introducing me to my editor, who brought this book to fruition.

Lastly, I am indebted to my editor, Tammy Wicks for her understanding, consideration, and wise counsel. She helped me in many ways. My appreciation and gratitude to her and all who helped her with my book.

About The Author

† Dr. (Rev) Willie D. McClung

Rev. Wille D. McClung, Ph.D. is a native of Alabama. His educational background is wide and varied. He holds as Associate, a Bachelor of Science, a Bachelor of Arts, and a Ph.D. from Wayne State University, Detroit, MI; Master of Arts, University of Detroit, Detroit, MI; Liberal Arts Curriculum, Miles College, Birmingham, AL, and Theology, Birmingham Baptist College, Birmingham, AL.

Some professional experiences include: Pastor, Holt Street Memorial Baptist Church, Montgomery, AL; Executive Director of the World Center, National Baptist Convention USA, Inc.; Vice President for Development, Selma University, Selma, AL; Instructor- Reading and Study Skills, Mississippi State University, Starkville, MS, and Instructor-Sociology, Psychology, Selma University, Selma, AL.

Rev. McClung is happily married to MaryJean McClung, and they have five children, David, Rosemary, Bonita, RaShon and LaDawn.

Professional Associations: Antioch District Association, Montgomery Baptist Minister's Union, Holt Street Baptist Church Historical Society, Eastside Kiwanis Club, etc. Honors: Leadership Award, Department of Housing, Birmingham, AL; Service Award, Miles College, Birmingham, AL; Outstanding Service Award, Mary Holmes College, West Point, MS; Leadership Award, State of Michigan;

Professional Associations (continued):

Montgomery Leadership Award, City of Highland Park, MI; Who's Who Among Black Americans, and Top Ten Students, Miles College, Birmingham, AL. Publications: "Black Baptist Pastors, The Black Baptist Church and Social Change: A Survey of Attitudes and Practices from Selected Churches in Detroit," "A Study of the Merger of Community Health Associated with Blue Cross Insurance," and "Who's Who in the National Baptist Convention, USA, Inc."

www.ingramcontent.com/pod-product-compliance
Lightning Source LLC
Chambersburg PA
CBHW070800230426
43665CB00017B/2432